CHRISTIANS ALIVE

Christians Alive

BRYAN GREEN

RECTOR OF BIRMINGHAM

CANON OF BIRMINGHAM CATHEDRAL

ENGLAND

CHARLES SCRIBNER'S SONS

NEW YORK

To
my daughter
JILL

Preface

THIS BOOK is intended for the ordinary man who wants to know something of what it means to be a Christian and to lead the Christian life. Thoughtful people have a right to be told what is implied in the demands of Christian discipleship before they are asked to make their surrender to Christ; not that anyone can possibly know all that it will mean before experiencing the new life that He gives. Young people in love, if they are wise, think out some of the implications of marriage before their wedding day, but they find, as many others have done, that afterwards they learn gradually how far-reaching are the full demands of love. Part of the tragedy of some broken marriages finds its origin precisely in this fact, that the couple never realized on what they were embarking. The all too common slackening off of zeal and loyalty of many Christians is frequently due to the same cause, that they did not understand enough about Christian discipleship before they entered into it.

The purpose of this book is in a modest fashion to seek to outline what it means to be a Christian in the world of today.

I do not know what is the experience of other writers on this subject. Mine has been an interesting one. To write about the Gospel and the glorious doctrine of justification by faith is a humbling experience; but it is humbling in quite a different way when one tries to write of Christian discipleship.

To speak of the Gospel, and to make plain the wonder of God's love which in Christ makes us sure that He takes us just as we are, accepts us sinners though we are, and unites us with Himself by His Spirit, is exhilarating. One is indeed humbled by the sense of one's own worthlessness, and the complete inadequacy of one's faith and gratitude in response to all that He has done, and all that He is. Certainly it convicts of sin; yet there is also an undertone of confidence and of sharing in the triumph of the Gospel. We glory in Christ and the wonder

9

of His redemption. Strangely we feel that in spite of what we are, we have a right, nay, an inescapable duty, to declare what we know, and to proclaim from the house-tops what Christ has done for us.

Writing about Christian discipleship and something of the meaning of Christian living also humbles us and convicts us of sin. We know how far short we fall of the ideals of the new life in Christ of which we write. There is, too, gratitude in our hearts that in any measure at all we have been able to live this life, but—and here is the difference—there is little sense that we must stand on the house-tops and proclaim the Christian life as we know it, or shout it aloud. We feel we represent our Master so poorly that we have little right to say anything very much about Christian living. It is a salutary experience, and I can only hope that what I have felt in this way comes out in what I have written.

I owe a debt of gratitude to friends of mine who have helped me in the writing of this book. To Bishop Stephen C. Neill, and to the late Canon B. K. Cunningham I am indebted for putting into my mind, more than twenty-five years ago, fruitful ideas which eventually have resulted in this book.

I am most grateful to three friends of mine who in the middle of their busy lives consented to read the manuscript, and whose suggestions and criticisms were most helpful and in many cases adopted. They are the Rev. Dr. James S. Stewart, Professor of New College, Edinburgh; the Dean of Liverpool, the Very Rev. F. W. Dillistone; and Canon G. H. Hewitt, Education Secretary in the Diocese of Sheffield.

I wish also to thank the Community of St. Julian's, near Horsham, for the truly holy and yet utterly joyful peace of their house in which, as with my first book, I had the privilege of staying while writing these chapters.

I close with an expression of thanks to my publishers for their help and courtesy, and as with my earlier book to my Secretary, Margery Northcott, for typing the book and preparing it for the Press.

BRYAN GREEN

The Rectory
Birmingham, England

Contents

CHAPTER I

Where Real Christianity Begins

IT was once said of a bishop: "He is so heavenly minded that he is no earthly use." Now, if our religion is so heavenly minded that it makes us no earthly use, then one thing is quite clear: whatever it is, it is not the true religion of Jesus Christ, because the first thing that a careful reader notices when he picks up the New Testament is that Christianity is a religion for this world as well as for the next. If we are going to be Christians, we have to be Christians in our own day and in our own generation. Christianity, therefore, cannot be just an other-worldly religion.

One of the happy changes that has come over the Churches during the last fifty years is a much more definite acceptance and a clearer understanding of what is implied by the Social Gospel. It is a commonplace today to which we all pay at least lip service, that religion has something to do with *this* life and *this* world, as well as to do with *that* life and *that* world. Yet it is important to make the point, because there is still far too much emasculated and weak Christianity—a pietism which seems to suggest that we turn to Christ mainly in order to be right for heaven. True though it is that we need to be prepared to die and to face the hereafter, for the world after death, if real, most certainly matters, we must see that it is even more urgent to be right with God in the present in order to live our life today.

It is true that the Bible continually emphasizes—and many modern Christians continually forget—ideas such as "your citizenship is in heaven." Of course it does, and rightly, for here we are being pointed forward to our final goal, the goal to which the true Christian genuinely looks forward, not simply living for this life with its short three score years and ten, but to the fuller life beyond time and space. That is our final goal, that is where we really belong as Christians, because that is where God most fully is, and where Christ reigns. "Where your treasure is, there will your heart be also." If we really love God then the life with God should be the place where our treasure is, and on which our heart's desire is focused.

When, however, we accept the fact that true Christianity has much to do with this life here and now we are not accepting anything easy. It is not possible, though some people try to do it, to turn to the New Testament, examine the example and teaching of Christ, and then transfer what we see there straight from first-century Palestine to twentieth-century America. We cannot say: "It was right and fitting then, so it is right and fitting now." First-century Palestine was quite different from our twentieth-century world, and therefore it is not very easy to make our Christianity relevant to this day and age.

On the one hand, I always think it is a little naïve when anybody says: "There is no argument. I can tell you how we ought to deal with the H-bomb (which is a twentieth-century phenomenon). Jesus said: 'If anybody hits you on one cheek, turn the other.' You can apply that straight away to the H-bomb. If anybody wants to drop an H-bomb on me, then I must take it, and if he wants to, he can drop another one. I am not going to do anything to protect myself."

Christian pacifism may or may not be right; but it cannot be rightly supported by this kind of argument. We cannot treat the New Testament and the teaching of Jesus in this fashion, and apply it to life today just like that.

On the other hand, there is an even greater danger, and that is to dismiss or water down the teaching of Jesus, and say it has nothing to do with life today. The basic principles of living that Jesus gave us, the spirit with which He lived, are as applicable today as they ever were. Our task, in order to make our Christianity relevant, is so to grasp with our own minds the spirit and mind of Jesus that we are able to bring them to bear on our life today. To try and see how that spirit and mind should work out in our own situations—that is the task before every real, thoughtful Christian.

I do not intend in these chapters to describe and analyse our twentieth-century situation; of such analyses we have far too many. There are, however, one or two aspects of our life today which need to be emphasized and recognized clearly before we can attempt to see how to live a positive Christian life. As the late William Temple said: "Modern man does not suffer, generally speaking, from much sense of guilt and shame; he does, however, suffer tremendously from a sense of frustration and powerlessness."

This is due, quite obviously, to the contradiction in which we find ourselves. On the one hand, the outstanding characteristic of our age is our scientific control of life, our amazing "know-how" in the managing of material forces and in the direction of our mental powers. We have never been so clever.

Against this fact we do not seem to have discovered the "know-how" for living together. As a President of the Royal Society for the Advancement of Science said a few years ago: "We are not good enough to be so clever." Of course this makes us frustrated and perplexed as soon as we stop to think sensibly about life today. On the one hand there are our scientific resources which would enable us to live amazingly well; has it not been said that our standards of living could be doubled in twenty years? On the other hand, we are living with a "cold war." Racial discrimination and segregation rear their ugly heads. Reasonable and true patriotism has given place to fierce and stupid nationalisms. The future certainly does not make a bright and happy prospect, if we are honest. We do not seem to be making any real progress in the art of personal relationships and of living together.

Where does our failure lie? The reasons, no doubt, are many and complex. Those who are not Christians will give different reasons from those who are; but I believe that at heart the real reason for our failure to live together as a human family is because we have forgotten our heavenly Father. Most certainly this is a godless age. Christendom, which once had some regard for the spiritual and the super-natural, has become already largely godless, while under the impact of our modern western civilization Africa and Asia seem to be losing their sense of the spiritual, and becoming in their turn godless.

This is the kind of world, this is the kind of thinking, in which we have to be Christians. We have to live amongst a mass of people who are, to all intents and purposes, practical atheists. This ungodliness, and this irreligion, create the situation we have to face. When General Omar Bradley said, "What we need is not more men of science, but more men of God" he was speaking the truth. But the men of God have got to be men of God in a world in which God has largely been forgotten. That quite precisely is the problem—how to live as a man of God in a world and in a society in which the majority deny the importance of God, and some even the existence of God.

This, from the Christian point of view, reveals the basic sin of our age, the sin of godlessness, and at the same time exposes the real source of our troubles and the cause of our bad personal relationships; and it is in this kind of godless and irreligious atmosphere that we must, if we are Christians, live as men and women of God.

The real challenge to us is to live as those in whose lives God really counts, to be men of faith and obedience to Him in a world that simply does not bother about Him at all. This is a supremely difficult life to live, because all the influences around us are saying to us, to use a modern colloquialism: "Fix it yourself; there is no need to call in God." But before we can live in this world as men of God we must first become for ourselves men of God, and this demands a radical and personal experience.

A man of God is a very definite kind of person. He cannot be easily defined or neatly identified, although he can be and ought to be clearly recognized as being a man of God. He is a man to whom God is real, in whose life God is the central force and the most important fact. He has had in some way a personal encounter with the Beyond, and in that encounter he has surrendered his will.

The nearest human analogy is that of a man in love. Many definitions have been attempted to explain what love is, and none is satisfactory. Those who observe others who love cannot neatly catalogue what constitutes that experience of loving. Those who are in love are certain that they are, but cannot adequately explain what they know and have experienced. Yet we can recognize, and what is more important, believe we should be able to recognize, a man in love. He too should know it, because if the experience is a valid one it should alter his behavior, lead to radical decisions, and shape his future life.

So it is with the man of God. In varying ways, as with the love experience, God has become real to him: to put it another way, he has experienced God in a vivid personal encounter. He knows it, and it has altered his life; or rather, he knows that it will alter his life, for the change may be sudden or it may be gradual. No one must seek to stereotype or dogmatize about the way of this experience, by what means it comes, or how it happens. If it is an authentic Christian experience of God a man will have encountered God in and through Jesus Christ. His awareness of God will be a discovery of a God who at one and the same time meets him with an absolute moral challenge as seen in the humanity of Jesus, and yet at the same moment offers him the forgiveness and help of a Savior-God who utterly loves him. From then on he will become a real Christian, or Christ's man.

Nicodemus, a churchman, once posed this question to Jesus Himself. "Lord, how do I become a man of God?"—that is partly what he meant in his discussion with Jesus about seeing the kingdom of God. Jesus' reply was strange and searching: "You have got to be born all over again. You know the facts of life—that which is born of the flesh is flesh. Nicodemus, you had a straightforward, honest-to-goodness human birth—that's how you arrived into this world." "Yes, indeed," replied Nicodemus; "I know that all right, but how can I possibly be born all over again." Jesus continued: "You will have to be if you want to become a man of God. Even if you can't grasp it with your mind it is an experience you must receive. Just as you had to be born physically to become a man, so you must be born of the Spirit to become a man of God. You need to have a real new life. As you had to begin your human life, so you have to begin your spiritual life. You must be born again."

This emphasis appears often in the teaching of Jesus. He was always making the point that the spiritual life, the life of the man of God, must have a beginning. He used metaphors like these: "Without God your life is as if you were dead—dead to God, God means nothing. When you have had the new birth you are alive to God—God now means something. Before this spiritual birth a man is lost, he is wandering away from God as the prodigal son wandered away. After the new birth he knows he has been found, found by the Father, and now he is at home, really at home, with God. Before that he was perishing, missing the mark; now he is saved, an integrated and real person." Paul, making the same point of the Christian Gospel, used other metaphors. Before our new birth, he tells us, we are enemies of God, self-willed and self-centered; afterwards we have become friends, reconciled.

I am not concerned to press the metaphors too far, but I am concerned to make perfectly plain the New Testament presupposition that somewhere there must be in my experience a personal encounter with God in Christ if I am to be a man of God as the New Testament understands a man of God. After all, it was to "save sinners" that Jesus Christ came. This new birth, this new life from God, is inseparably linked with the coming of Christ. He came to die upon the Cross under the impact of our sin, to show God's love in face of our sin, God's hatred of our sin, and to suffer for our sin. On the first Easter Day He rose again victorious to show here on the stage of history that God's love and goodness are the real spiritual power behind the world.

Yet all this is not enough. These are only the historic facts. Christ did come on the first Christmas Day; He did die on the first Good Friday; He did rise on the first Easter Sunday;

but it was not until Pentecost, the first Whit Sunday, that the Spirit of God, who is just like Jesus, entered men's and women's hearts, making Christ real to them, and giving them the new birth, the new life in Christ, so that they became in the Christian sense men and women of God.

In every discussion about the new birth it cannot be said too often or too plainly that it is the *fact* of the new birth that matters, and not the date or the method. In spite of the clearest teaching about this there is still much misunderstanding. We must walk carefully between Scylla and Charybdis. We must not make the Christian experience so vague and shadowy and ill-defined that we distort it into a general religiosity; nor, on the other hand, must we define it so clearly that it seems that only with certain emotional accompaniments can it happen. The deepest human personal relationship is the only adequate analogy here. Consider the experience of falling in love. There is what may be called, somewhat inexactly, love at first sight—a dramatic and definite encounter between two persons who discover that they were meant for each other, discover it with some emotion, at a definite time, in a definite place.

To others the love experience comes differently. They have many attempts on several occasions, they fancy it is true love, then discover it was a passing fancy or a temporary infatuation. After some time of despair and disillusionment they try again, until finally true love enters their lives.

Thirdly, there are those who met in childhood as family friends; the friendship deepened, until later on they almost slipped into the experience of love, discovering that what began as friendship had passed beyond; friends for years, they were now lovers.

These illustrations are always inexact, but the three ways cover, roughly speaking, how men and women fall in love. It does not matter in which way it happens. It is essentially a definite experience: "We are in love." It is a conscious experience: "We know we are in love." It is a life-changing experience: "We want to be married."

So it is with the new birth. It may come with a dramatic,

sudden crisis at a point of time and in a certain place, with conviction of sin, and with an emotional struggle. I am met by the Living Christ, and I have to say yes or no to Him. Such are often the converts at mass evangelistic rallies.

Again, for others there is a long intellectual and moral struggle. Such a man often thinks he has become a real Christian, that he really can now believe the Christian Faith. Then he finds that he has not yet arrived. At length, after years of striving, he finds Christ and is found by Him.

Again, there is a third group who are fortunate enough to be brought up in a true Christian home, perhaps baptized in infancy, later received into full Church membership, living after the pattern of Christian ethics. Such people often slip almost imperceptibly into the new life. Their spiritual rebirth is almost unconscious, for there is little or no emotional or moral struggle.

What needs to be said, and said quite plainly, is that it is of no importance whatever in which of the three ways I enter into the new life in Christ. It is certainly a definite experience: "I am a man in Christ." It is conscious: "I know I am His." It is life-changing: "I desire to be led by His Spirit day by day."

Keeping this analogy in mind, we see that just as the love experience ushers in the married life, so the new birth is only the beginning; after this beginning there must be a continuing. Those who rightly emphasize conversion to Christ must also emphasize continuance in Christ. After the new birth we are meant to grow in grace, and in the knowledge of Jesus Christ our Lord and Savior; and it is this Christian life which is the real witness to the truth and relevance of the Gospel.

None the less in Church circles today, in spite of all the evangelism in the last decades, it is still necessary to assert that a man cannot live the Christian life until he has first become a real Christian. It is still quite possible to be a churchgoer without ever being truly born again. It is still possible to try to follow the code of Christian behavior without God being the living, central fact of life. It is still possible to receive the Sacrament without knowing the Savior, and to come to the Communion without coming to Christ. It is still possible to make a regular practice of worshipping in church without the opening of the heart and the submission of the will to the God whom we profess to worship.

CHAPTER II

The Basis of Certainty

THE Christian life is meant to have a certain quality or temper inherent within it. The Christian disciple should have certain marks which bear witness that he is indeed a man of God. J. B. Phillips in his preface to the Acts of the Apostles remarks that one fact stood out in his mind in the course of his translation work: and that was the vitality of New Testament Christian living, and the amazing contrast between it and that of much modern Christian discipleship. The Christian Church in the New Testament, in spite of many faults and failures, in spite of human imperfections and sins, throbs with vitality. Here there is enthusiasm, initiative, drive, creativeness; it is indeed a new phenomenon in human history. G. K. Chesterton notices the same fact, and describes the New Testament Christian as a person who feels himself to be "carrying about a key to life," and the Christian Church as a "winged thunderbolt of everlasting enthusiasm, as new as it is old."

One reason for this vitality was, and still should be, that the first note of the Christian life is *a life of certainty*. The Christian is meant to know that he is a real Christian; he is not meant to be a prey to doubts, fears and anxieties about the reality of his religion. In the New Testament again and again we find emphasis laid upon the word "know." "We *know* that we have passed from death unto life, because we love the brethren."[1] "I *know* whom I have believed, and am persuaded that he is able to keep that which I have committed unto him

[1] 1 John 3:14

22

against that day."[2] "Hereby we know that he abideth in us."[3] "This is life eternal, that they might know thee the only true God, and Jesus Christ, whom thou hast sent."[4] So the quotations could be multiplied. The whole climate of the New Testament religion is the climate of certainty, of certainty about God and a personal experience of Him. Paul perhaps sums it up most beautifully in the grand passage in Philippians where he says: "I count all things but loss for the excellency of the knowledge of Christ Jesus my Lord . . . that I may win Christ, and be found in him . . . that I may know him, and the power of his resurrection."[5]

From this certainly two characteristic emotions of the New Testament emerge. The early Christians were a joyful community. Paul, writing to his friends from prison, talked a great deal about joy, and urged them continually to "rejoice in the Lord." Here was no superficial happiness nor freedom from a measure of sorrow; for many Christians they were dark days of persecution, misunderstanding, of loneliness and fear; but so certain were they of God that their inner joy remained.

The other emotion was hope. At first glance they had little for which to hope; for were they not a motley crowd, most of them of the poorer, less educated classes, despised and harried? Yet they were full of hope, not in the least because they were certain of themselves, of their faith, of the success of their efforts, but because they were certain of God and of what He could do through them. Such Christians, if they were here today, would have been, in face of militant communism and secular atheism, full of hope and joy, because they were not only certain of their own personal knowledge of God in Christ, but because they were certain that this God whom they knew was the Lord of all life, and that the kingdoms of this world in the end would become the kingdoms of their God and of His Christ. That is a fair description of the New

[2] 2 Timothy 1:12
[3] 1 John 3:24
[4] John 17:3
[5] Philippians 3:8

Testament Christian. Is it not lamentably true that amongst modern Christians today this note of certainty is largely absent?

We must, however, understand what is meant by Christian certainty. In the strict philosophical sense it is not absolute certainty; it is better described as a probable certainty, but none the less it is such a probable certainty that our lives can be based upon it.

Here is a happily married man who is away from his wife across the seas. He does not wake up in the morning, immediately put through a transatlantic call and speak to his wife over the phone, anxiously asking her: "Darling, do you love me?" He is certain of that, just as certain of that as he could be about anything in his life; and there is no presumption in this certainty. Doubtless in the strict philosophical sense he has no absolute certainty; he may be making a mistake; all these years he may have misinterpreted the meaning of all that his wife has said, has done, has been; but the absence of absolute certainty does not worry him; in his own mind he has a probable certainty that on all the evidence his wife does love him, and that their personal relationship is secure. He is, therefore, freed from all anxiety and worry about that fact, and he lives his life happily based on a probable certainty.

Moreover, it is important to observe that this probable certainty in his wife's love is not shaken by the fact that, as all sensible people are, he is fully aware of his own shortcomings, his failures to be the perfect husband, to return adequately the love he is so freely given. This undoubtedly produces a sense of humility and gratitude, but it doesn't shake his certainty of his wife's love.

So it is with our knowledge of God in Christ. Our certainty of Him should take away all anxiety, doubt and fear, and enable us to say with St. Paul, that "we know Him in whom we have believed."

Another point that must be made clear is that this certainty of our relationship with God in Christ does not free us from doubts about the Christian faith, nor about many aspects of Christian living. As a matter of fact, I am inclined to think that a measure of doubt is a necessary ingredient in Christian progress. The Christian life has its times of shadow. "Lord, I believe, help Thou my unbelief" can be a truly Christian prayer. Further by way of a rough illustration we can divide Christians into two groups, both of whom enjoy a genuine Christian experience. There are those who have what is called "a simple faith," and who never worry intellectually about their Christianity. My Mother is like that—a wonderful Christian both in her inner personal religion, and in the witness of her active living. She knows and loves her Savior, and has never had any intellectual doubts or questioning about her faith. She was quite unable to understand my doubts and difficulties, and could not see why I should be worried: "It's just a matter of faith." Such Christians are people of great spiritual power; they are the salt of the earth. We cannot argue with them—in fact, we do not wish to. They know—and we know they know.

On the other hand, there is a second group of Christians who, because of their mental make-up must think things out, and who cannot have convictions unless these convictions make sense to them. In their own way they are trying to carry out their Lord's injunction. "Thou shalt love the Lord thy God with all thy mind." Having minds, they have to use them to think about their religion. It is not true to suggest that such Christians want to prove everything; they know there is much that never can be proved. It is not that they want to have a nice, watertight explanation for all God's ways with men; but it is that they must think about all that interests them, and therefore about God who interests them most of all. Such thinking inevitably brings to mind a series of doubts and question marks. I remember the late Canon Streeter once saying to me at a lunch: "If you settle the answer before you start to think, you can't think." That chance remark was a great help to me as a student, for I soon found that if I did not settle the answer beforehand, but started to think with an open mind, I was really thinking. Sometimes, of course, I landed myself into doubts or found answers which afterwards turned out to be wrong, and so forth, but I was really thinking. . . .

But for many Christians this is a necessary element if they are to be real, live and thinking Christians. But deeper than these doubts and questions should be the certainty of Christ, though this certainty does not free us from a large measure of intellectual doubt.

Moreover, it is possible to be certain about God, and yet very uncertain from time to time about His guidance. Recall my analogy of husband and wife. It is true that in the early days of marriage, while certain of each other's love, they may often be uncertain about each other's wishes. The experience of living together will tend to correct this, so that after a long married life each may instinctively know the other's will, but even then there may still be some measure of uncertainty. So it is with our experience of God. In time, through coming to understand more truly the spirit and mind of Jesus, we can be fairly sure of the general will of God, but in matters of guidance day by day we are left often extremely uncertain as to how He wants us to act, or what He wishes us to do.

Furthermore, assured as we can be about our personal relationship with God, we can still be a prey to much anxiety and to much questioning about our own spiritual state and progress in discipleship. Most of us know what it is sadly to wonder whether we are making any progress in the Christian life, whether we are becoming deeper Christians, or whether perhaps we are slipping away from a spiritual level to which God has brought us. In all this there is plenty of room for doubts and uncertainties and questionings, but underneath them all we can have the privilege of a strong certainty of our standing with God as His forgiven, redeemed children.

On what can this certainty be based? It must not depend upon anything subjective in us, for we are fickle and change too easily. Therefore, neither my feelings nor my behavior as I observe them can be the guarantee of my personal relationship with God.

The first ground of my assurance is fairly and squarely the character of God Himself. It is sometimes expressed in the words, "We rest on the promises of God," but this is liable to misunderstanding. That is why it is better to state the doctrine of assurance as Paul himself does in the Epistle to the Romans, resting it upon the basis of what God is and eternally will be. Let me illustrate, by the use of a text much used in evangelism: "Behold, I stand at the door and knock. If any man hear my voice and open the door, I will come in to him."[6] Countless thousands of men and women have found this text a focus point for their faith. Its simple picture language enables us to open the door and receive Christ as Savior and Lord. Then it offers encouragement to believe Christ's promise, and to find assurance that He has entered. It may be put like this: "You have heard His voice; you have known that God is calling you; you have been convicted of your need for Him; you want Him in your life—that is hearing His voice. You are willing by an act of will to change your mind, to repent, and in the simple trust of faith to ask Him to enter your life, to come as your forgiving Savior, to take control as your Master—now you have opened the door. How do you know that He has entered? How do you know that He has brought you into a new relationship with Himself?" Because He has promised: "I will come in, and you believe His promise."

This is perfectly true, and as I have said, thousands of true Christians throughout the world have found an assurance of God and His forgiveness through some such promise of scripture. But the ground of assurance should not really be allowed to rest just here. What lies behind those words, "I will come in"? We cannot find a genuine certainty of God from a few words in printer's ink on India paper in a book called the Bible. Behind these words stands the whole fact of Christ, and all that God's act in history in Him has declared about the character of God who has so acted. Behind these words stands the Christ who died on the Cross for sinners; behind these words stands the Christ who as a living Savior has entered and changed human lives ever since by His Spirit.

So then, my certainty rests not on a few Bible texts or promises, valuable though they are, nor even on any one particular event in history, splendid and revealing though that may be;

[6] Revelation 3:20

it rests upon the eternal, unchanging God who in Christ has declared once and for all and unmistakably that He is righteous, but yet loves and forgives the sinner. That is our certainty. More than that faith cannot demand; and less than that would not satisfy.

Secondly, our certainty rests upon the covenant of God, especially His covenant as revealed in the Sacrament of Baptism. Here we are reminded again of the Old Testament covenant days, with the thought of "covenant" initiating us into a new relationship. In our baptism we are baptized into the death of Christ. With Paul's words in Romans Chapter 6 in mind we can picture a flowing river, beside which a man stands awaiting baptism. The water represents the redeeming blood of Christ, that is to say, God's redeeming, forgiving love for the sinner. It is ever flowing, flowing even before the man goes down to be baptized in it; it flows ceaselessly, and it flows always, and it flows for everyone. Into that flood the man steps; it envelops him, cleanses him, redeems him. He is identified thus with the blood of Christ, united with Christ by the love of God, and comes out to live a new life in a new relationship with God through the power of the Risen Christ. That outward baptism of water is the sacrament, the outward and visible sign of the inward and spiritual reality of his new life, of his dying to sin and becoming alive to God in Christ.

In this way our certainty rests upon the covenant of God expressed in baptism. Because, however, many of us have been baptized as infants something else must be said. The Christian experience is a fully personal relationship between God and man. It can never, from one point of view, be a one-sided relationship. True, in infant baptism God's love takes the initiative; but it awaits a conscious response. God's offer calls for my acceptance. All that infant baptism stands for is completed, in the Anglican Church (to which I belong), at Confirmation, and in other Churches by some other form of outward avowal of faith. Our fully completed baptism, then, becomes part of the ground of our assurance. Luther found his certainty by looking back and saying: "I have been baptized." If God's covenant means anything, then we are in covenant relationship with Him through baptism; we are among those whom He has redeemed by his precious blood. This is the second ground of assurance.

The third is the conviction of the Spirit. "The Spirit himself beareth witness with our spirits that we are the children of God." We must remember that this conviction of the Spirit is not a kind of feeling, an inward sense that I am all right. It is, rather, a deep inner conviction based upon evidence that the Holy Spirit is working in my life. I believe that all real Christians should be able to look at themselves, and with humility see that the Holy Spirit is bearing witness to their relationship with God.

What is the evidence for which we should look? It is not primarily that our behavior is becoming more Christlike, though indeed this should be so; it is, rather, evidence that Jesus Christ is coming to mean more and more to us. It was Jesus Himself who said that one of the signs that the Holy Spirit is working within us would be that Christ would be "glorified." What exactly does this mean?

The word "glory" in the New Testament often suggests the real nature of a person as seen, or revealed. For instance, we read: "God . . . hath shined in our hearts, to give the light of the knowledge of the glory of God in the face of Jesus Christ."[7] Here the thought is surely that God reveals to a person, and gives to him, the knowledge of something of His own real nature, and this real nature is seen in Christ. When our Lord refers to the Holy Spirit glorifying Him, I think He means that as the Holy Spirit works in our lives we shall come to understand more of the person of Christ, and He will come to have more meaning for us.

Everybody has his own experience, but my own is something like this. Travelling about the world, as I have had the privilege and opportunity of doing, I naturally meet hundreds of professing Christians. As I get to know some of them reasonably intimately and we talk about religion, they tend to fall into two groups. The first make me uncertain as to whether they are

[7] 2 Corinthians 4:6

real Christians or not. It is not my business to judge them, and I refuse to allow my mind to say to me, "These are not Christians," but a question mark which I cannot prevent is raised in my mind.

The other group leave me in no doubt. The underlying note in their religion, the deep undertone constantly sounding, is a Christ-centeredness. Inevitably, just as the compass-needle swings to the magnetic North, so their point of reference is Jesus Christ Himself.

One of the points that troubles me about much religious talk today is the over-emphasis on the word "Church." As I hope to make clear in a later chapter, I do not believe that the real Christian life is possible outside the Church, and that the Church is not an extra, but a necessity. Nevertheless, I am unhappy when I hear people talking about the Church when I feel that they should be talking about Christ. I think there is a danger of overworking Paul's metaphor of the Church as the Body of Christ. It is a good metaphor, especially as he makes it quite clear that Christ is the Head of the body; both head and body are important, but if you press the metaphor, then I should claim that the head controls the body, and it is the head that matters more than the body. Similarly, the Church is the Body and reflects the mind and spirit of Christ here on earth; it should be a tool and instrument for His Spirit. None the less Christ is the Head of His Church, and we should give Him His pre-eminence both in our thinking and in our speaking.

I realize that in life's actual experience we cannot separate God from His world, or Christ from His Church, but in explanation and in speaking there is a distinction here, and if we do not make it we tend to blur the essential reality of Christ. It is particularly dangerous, because there is no doubt that it is all too possible to be a "churchy" Christian, one to whom the Church is the center, and not Christ. This is the kind of Christian of whom Karl Barth wrote: "They are dangerous by-products and regrettable misunderstandings."

If, therefore, we find our minds naturally turning toward Christ when we think of our religion or when we think of

God, then perhaps we can believe that in some measure the Holy Spirit is bearing witness within us that we are true children of God.

These, then, are the grounds of the Christian's assurance and happy certainty—the character of God, the covenant of God, and a deep conviction about Christ.

CHAPTER III

A Life of Tension

THESE days we are told we are living a life of tension, and that our great need is to relax. For many people tranquillizing pills seem a necessity, or, if we can afford it, the psychiatrist's couch. To a large extent this is true, for the pace and pressure of modern life does indeed produce much nervous tension, and to learn how to relax, and then how to find refreshment of mind and spirit, is a lesson that all of us must learn. It will, therefore, sound surprising when I suggest that the second mark of the Christian life is that it is *a life of tension*. Here I am not using the word in the sense of nervous tension, but rather in the sense of a life strung taut between two opposite truths. It is something like a piece of elastic stretched taut between two points, and in that tautness is the real way of life. Let me explain.

The first focus-point is the peace of God, the serenity of which the Bible so often speaks. One of the first fruits of the work of the Holy Spirit in our hearts is that we are given the peace that passes all understanding. Jesus Himself promised it to us when He said: "My peace I leave with you; my peace I give unto you." Christian hymns are full of the idea, so are other Christian writings. When a man is right with God, then he is possessed by a deep inner serenity of heart and conscience. It is the hall-mark of the true Christian. If I were forced to choose one characteristic of a real saint it would be this serenity of mind, grounded in a deep, inner and abiding relationship with God.

When I was a boy one of my aunts made a great impression on me, and as I grew into maturity she made an even greater impression. I often think she was one of the very few real and special saints I have ever met. She was a remarkable woman, educated and cultured, and violently evangelical. Her ordinary conversation and phraseology were strongly biblical. If she had not been a real saint no one for one moment would have tolerated what I can only describe as her overweening pietism, but because of this deep inner serenity and sincerity one could take from her phrases and ideas which would have been nauseating if anyone else had used them.

Before the first World War she had a Bible class for London policemen. They hung on every word as she taught them Sunday by Sunday. As a schoolboy during the first World War I saw her manage a canteen full of soldiers; she talked to them about religion; they listened spell-bound, though her phrases and words were completely biblical.

Between the wars I introduced her once to a group of sophisticated young society women, smartly dressed and thoroughly worldly. My aunt was drab and dowdy. Within five minutes she had them eating out of her hand. She spoke to them of Christ.

On one occasion she was hurrying to catch a train at Paddington Station. Arriving dead on time she found the barrier gate slammed in her face. Out aloud she ejaculated, beaming all over her face: "Never mind. Praise the Lord." Then she went off to get a cup of tea. On returning for the next train, the ticket collector said: "Excuse me, Ma'am. What was that you said when I slammed the door in your face half an hour ago?" "I don't remember," she replied. "It sounded strange to me. Did you say something like 'Praise the Lord'?" My aunt paused a moment, and then answered: "Yes, I expect I did. I do praise Him. I am sure it is quite all right that I missed the train, and God has some purpose for me through it." To her surprise the ticket collector asked: "Would you mind missing another train, because I should like to speak to you after this one has gone." So she missed another train, and he told her his story, the story of a marriage breaking up, of his longing for help, and before she caught her train she had helped him to put his faith in Christ, and later to put his marriage right.

The idea I am trying to underline is that this natural—and I emphasize the word "natural"—serenity of mind and spirit is the hall-mark of a genuine Christian experience. That must be one focus-point in our Christian life.

The second focus-point is equally important, and if we do not live like a piece of elastic stretched taut between these two points then serenity alone would lead us to pietism and escapism. Let me illustrate.

Some years ago I was the main speaker at a students' conference. It was organized by a remarkably fine group of students, full of evangelistic zeal, and thoroughly sensible. Because they were good mixers they had managed to bring to the conference with them a number of their friends who were agnostics, atheists, and a few Communists. During the open session, as I sat at the back listening, I realized we were in for a heated discussion. A delightful young medical student was in the chair, and he invited the Christians to stand up and say what Christ meant to them. This a number did, most sincerely, but not very convincingly. One after the other they got up and said that now that Christ had come into their lives they were so happy. I knew there would be an explosion. One of the Communists got up and shouted: "You Christians make me sick. Here you are gloating about your wretched little happiness in a world of exploitation and evil," and then he went on to expatiate on the social evils that needed putting right. The chairman hastily got up, and interrupting him, said: "I think we had better move on to something more practical."

This underlines the second focus-point. It is that along with an inner serenity there must come to us a divine discontent— discontent with evil, wherever it is in God's world. True Christian living consists in the tautness or tension between inner peace and divine discontent. If we are Christians we have no right to say: "God's in His heaven, all's right with the world." All is not right with the world, even though God's in His heaven—and that is what brings the tension.

Paul expounds this very clearly when he says: "The love of God is shed abroad in our hearts by the Holy Ghost which is given unto us."[1] Here the love of God is a subjective genitive. It does not mean our love for God, but refers to God's own love. Something of God's own divine love is given to us by the Holy Spirit. When He takes hold of us then within us is born something of His own divine love, and this inevitably creates divine discontent.

In that wonderful chapter in Isaiah we read: "He shall see of the travail of his soul, and be satisfied"[2]—but He is not satisfied here and now with the world as it is. Jesus wept over Jerusalem because of the evil and disobedience that He saw. So when we are united with Christ we, too, must share in the fellowship of His sufferings; we must accept a deep and real discontent of mind and heart—discontent with our own sin and our own weakness; discontent with the evil and follies of the world. We must learn to hate all that ruins and spoils God's world, and hurts his children. To be really concerned and to find the burden of the sin intolerable are part and parcel of being a real Christian.

Here, then, is the tension—on the one hand it is easy to try to forget the evils of the world, and to practise a pietistic escapism by rejoicing in our own happiness and in our own peace with God. On the other hand, it is all too easy to rush into the world moved by divine discontent to try to change things by humanitarian philanthropy, losing as we do it our inner serenity, and the power which comes from it. It is a mark of Christian maturity to maintain the tension, and to hold both truths vividly alive in our hearts at the same time.

Masefield in his *Everlasting Mercy* preserves this tension perfectly:

> *I did not think, I did not strive,*
> *The deep peace burnt my me alive;*
> *The bolted door had broken in,*
> *I knew that I had done with sin.*
> *I knew that Christ had given me birth*
> *To brother all the souls on earth,*

[1] Romans 5:5
[2] Isaiah 53:11

And every bird and every beast,
Should share the crumbs broke at the feast.[3]

Dr. Billy Graham in his preaching often says: "It is easy to be a Christian." I know what he means, and he is perfectly right. Because God's forgiveness in Christ is a gift it is simple to accept. To take the gift offered is what anyone can do. But we must not twist this perfectly true remark to mean what Dr. Graham never meant it to suggest, namely, that Christianity is easy. The Christian life is difficult; it is a very costly business to live it properly, and part of that cost is the willingness to live in a continual tension between serenity and discontent.

To put it rather differently: We are ambassadors for Christ in an alien world. To put it somewhat differently again: We are meant to share in God's redemptive purpose, and no one can redeem anyone else without strain and stress and struggle. It is possible to enter into life to redeem it possessed with a sense of peace and serenity, but in the very struggle our hands get dirty because we are identified with that which we are seeking to redeem. This very involvement with evil situations produces the discontent and the strain about which I am writing.

Some years ago in America a graduate of one of the Universities was converted to Christ. The next day she gave me a poem she had written. Whether as poetry the verses are good or bad is of no consequence, but the thought expresses exactly what I have been trying to say:

Yesterday I longed for something intangible,
For a way, an escape—
For the fulfilment of my longing.
I looked at the sky
And wished it would swallow me;
Wrap me in its myriad clouds
And give me peace.
I wanted only to sleep—
To be insensible

[3] John Masefield, *Poems*, New York: The Macmillan Company, 1958, p. 118. Used by permission of The Macmillan Company, New York, The Society of Authors, London, and Dr. John Masefield, O.M.

To love—to feel no more.
But today I have found reality.
My eyes have been opened
And I long no more.
Christ has come—
He has fulfilled His promise,
I am complete.
He knocked at my heart's threshold,
I answered—
He walked in.
Now I wish to live—
To serve Him—
Never to shut my eyes—
Never to escape—
I am caught in the light,
Darkness holds no fear.
But I do not want it.
The sky is a distant haven,
It is near and living,
It is comfort, solace, beauty.
I want to see life
To recognize its dirt
And help to clean it.
I want to speak
To let the living Saviour
Use my lips, my heart, my brain,
To bring others to his way.
He suffered mortal anguish—
He overcame it—
He bore the burden,
And now he offers
Forgiveness as His gift.
He has come—
I am complete—
The promise is fulfilled.

CHAPTER IV

A Life of Daily Communion

IF Christian discipleship is a personal relationship with the living God, then one of its marks must be that of *a life of daily communion* with the One whom we claim to love. It is true that in one sense our relationship with God in Christ is a once-for-all relationship—that is my certainty; but it is also a developing relationship to be continually maintained, and continually deepened. This we will call the third mark of the Christian life.

This the Bible makes very plain. We have "boldness to enter into the holy place by the blood of Jesus."[1] It is our right and privilege every day, because of God's love to us in Christ, to go into the holy place of His presence with the same freedom and spontaneity with which a child communicates with his father. We can talk to God with confidence and with love, looking up and saying: "Abba, Father."

This emphasis on simple daily communion with God is necessary, because we can so easily depersonalize God. Consider that New Testament phrase, "the grace of God." Grace is never an impersonal thing, and yet one often hears grace spoken about as if it is a thing that can be stored up as if it were a kind of celestial electricity. I made this point once at a meeting, and afterwards one of my audience produced a book, *A Guide to the First Communion*, in which there was a reference to a "reserve of grace," and readers were encouraged to go to the Holy Communion in order to store up grace for the rest of the week. I understand what the writer was trying to say, but there is a danger in the way in which he said it.

[1] Hebrews 10:19

Grace, in the Bible, is not impersonal. It points to a God who acts graciously. It is the gracious activity of God Himself, and we cannot store up God in a reservoir and, as it were, turn Him on when we need Him. It sounds almost blasphemous when written down in black-and-white, but there are many Christians who unconsciously think like this. They seem to believe that if they practise certain religious acts at a certain time then they can store up enough spiritual help—this impersonal stuff called grace—in a kind of reservoir inside themselves, so that when, for instance, on Monday they meet a strong temptation at 40-lb pressure they can stand up to it because they have 80-lb pressure of grace stored up within them, and then they will still have another 40-lb stored up for another emergency. Then next Sunday, having exhausted their supply, they can replenish their store and start again.

No Christian would put it exactly like this, I know, but it is a very prevalent attitude, and a very dangerous one. Before we know where we are we shall find ourselves back again under law, and in bondage to legalism. We shall find ourselves trying to perform certain acts at certain times thinking that by so doing we shall earn or collect spiritual power and grace. This utterly distorts the glorious fact of our personal relationship with God. We are either daily in touch with Him, or we are not. If we are, then He is there to help us all the time and in everything. "Jesus Christ is the same yesterday and today, yea and for ever."[2] "I will never leave thee, nor forsake thee. So that we may boldly say, The Lord is my helper, and I will not fear what man shall do unto me."[3] That confident assertion of Paul's, "My grace is sufficient for thee: for my strength is made perfect in weakness,"[4] means, when we paraphrase it, that Christ is saying to Paul: "I, the gracious One, will always be sufficient to meet your needs, so that when you feel utterly weak then my strength is fully at your disposal." Here is a real personal dependence of man upon God, a dependence which rests upon a daily and continuing inner communion.

[2] Hebrews 13:8
[3] Hebrews 13:5
[4] 2 Corinthians 12:9

The experience of Christians through the centuries has underlined some of the ways by which this daily communion is best maintained. In a human friendship the relationship is maintained and deepened by talking to each other, by listening to each other, by working with each other, and simply by being with each other. So man's communion with God is developed. Prayer becomes an essential part of Christian living. There is no rule or regulation that prayers must be said every day, and that if this rule is broken we sin. From the point of view of law there is no commandment about praying. Even the teaching of the Bible about saying prayers, and the encouragement of our Lord to "ask and you shall receive," are not so much commandments laid down for us to obey as practical and wise advice which we shall ignore at our spiritual peril. It is plain from our Lord's own practice, as well as from His teaching, that if we do not pray regularly, then we shall not maintain and deepen our daily communion with God; that is why daily prayer is a habit we learn to accept for ourselves through experience rather than a commandment laid down by authority. It is obvious that unless I consciously turn my mind and spirit toward God at regular intervals, then under the pressure of daily life I shall find myself out of touch with Him.

The reason that I am stressing this attitude to prayer is because some Christians find themselves in bondage to rules and regulations about praying. All of us need a habit or plan for daily prayer, because we are weak and feeble creatures of time and sense; we need, therefore, the discipline of setting apart a time and place for deliberately and consciously turning toward God in prayer. But it should be a spontaneous desire to keep in communion with our Lord that should prompt us to keep this time and place for praying rather than that we should feel bound by some rule or regulation.

One of the encouraging signs in Christian literature during the last thirty or forty years has been the publication both of books of prayers, and of helps in the art of prayer. The Christian who wants to learn to pray better will have no difficulty at all in finding a suitable guide to help him to attain his object.

Bible-reading is another way of maintaining our communion

with God, and here again during recent decades much help has been given by books both on the Bible itself, and on Bible-reading. Every serious student of the Bible should be able to find something that will give him just what he requires. There are, however, a few general principles that I wish to underline.

First, we must remember that we do not read the Bible primarily to seek from it rules of conduct, though indeed it contains admirable rules of conduct. Nor do we read it primarily to inform our minds about the Christian faith, although it is obvious that no one can discover the Christian faith except through the Bible. We read the Bible first and foremost in order that through the Bible God may speak to us. When Peter was telling Cornelius of the Gospel, we are told: "The Holy Spirit descended on them all as they heard the Word behind his words."[5] As we read the Scriptures we seek to hear the Word of God behind the printed words.

I find the doctrine of the inspiration of the Bible a difficult one, and the question of the authority of the Bible is no easy intellectual problem. Throughout the history of the Christian Church Christians have differed not only in their interpretation of the Scriptures, but also about such matters as historicity, infallibility and authority. These are important points, and I do not wish in the least to suggest that they do not matter, or that they can be by-passed by the Christian Church and by Christian scholars. It is, however, true in the experience of all Christians everywhere and always that when we go sincerely to the Bible wanting to hear the word of God, He does speak to us in the Scriptures as He seems to speak to us in no other way. The authoritative word of God comes to us through the Bible. Because of this fact Christians have always found that if they want to deepen their communion with God, and to progress in the Christian life, the reading of the Scriptures is essential. That is why both in public worship in the various liturgies a generous place is given to the reading of the Scriptures, and

[5] Acts 10:44 (Rieu's translation)

also in private, individual Christians are encouraged regularly to read the Bible.

In my experience both of evangelistic and of pastoral work I have become convinced that nothing is more important for the new convert and the young Christian beginner than to learn to know the Scriptures. By this I do not mean reading books about the Bible, or books on Christian doctrine based on the Bible; I mean reading the Bible itself. While I regard each book of the Bible as having its own special place in the volume of the Scriptures, and therefore in a sense necessary to the understanding of the whole, there are clearly some books more urgently important than others.

For the new convert the Epistles—letters specially written for new converts—are perhaps the part that should be read first. Yet we must remember that the Gospels are equally important, for here and here alone is the authentic record of the person and life of Christ.

This conviction as to the need for Bible-reading has nothing to do with churchmanship. The late Fr. Algy Robertson, a Franciscan monk, and I often met at conferences for young people. It always caused us a certain amount of amusement to see which of us would be the first to recommend regular Bible study-groups as an essential for Christian growth. This emphasis may appear unnecessary, but it is surprising and distressing to notice in how many local churches of all denominations there seems to be an almost complete absence of regular Bible study-groups. This is a matter which urgently needs to be remedied.

When I was first ordained I had the privilege of starting and leading a Sunday afternoon meeting for secondary-school boys and girls between the ages of fourteen and nineteen. The attendance ranged between 250 and 300 each week. Perhaps the most significant activity was on a Wednesday morning at seven o'clock, winter and summer alike, when anything up to eighty would gather before school for half an hour that we might read our Bibles together. There was nothing elaborate in our study; we just read the Bible from the point where we left off the week before, and let the Word of God speak to us. What is required? A Bible, with nice large print; a pencil, to mark passages that specially grip; and then let the Bible speak. It is almost as simple as that. There is room for the use from time to time of a good commentary, and of real, pains-taking study of the Bible to supplement the work in a Bible study-group, and to enrich daily private devotional reading of Bible passages; but I am sure from my experience there is need to grasp this basic principle of turning to the Bible to allow God to speak to us.

I owe this insight to my father-in-law who often spoke at religious conferences. When I was engaged we used to have some hours together frequently during my vacations, and then we turned to the Bible. He read it, and without bothering about commentaries, or spending undue time on difficult words and phrases, he let the Word speak to us. We tried to understand what the Bible was saying to us, and then we listened for God's word.

Once we can grasp this attitude to the Bible, and use it as we read, then it does not matter very much what pattern or plan we have for our daily Bible-reading, or for our deeper study. We shall be in the attitude when the Bible will help us to maintain our daily communion with our Lord.

Another way of deepening our personal relationship with God is the Holy Communion. If one seriously surveys the experience of the Christian Church from its birth until now, it is impossible to escape the conviction that of all the ways by which Christian people have deepened their communion with their Lord the way above all others has been the sacramental feeding upon the Body and Blood of Christ at the Lord's Supper. This is true not only when we look at the experience of the Roman Catholic and the Eastern Orthodox Churches, but also when we turn to the Reformed Communions. Think of the place given, on the one hand, to this Sacrament by the Lutherans, by the Anglicans and by the Presbyterians; and also, for instance, by the Brethren, whose main service each Sunday morning is the Breaking of Bread.

I am not concerned either with the form of service in which the Sacrament is taken, or with the frequency of the taking, but rather with the fact that Christians of all the Churches recognize that here, and here pre-eminently, is an act by which our communion with God is maintained. It is a pity that this great Sacrament, which is meant to bind us together in fellowship as one body in Christ, and which, as experience shows, was given to us by our Lord to deepen and strengthen our communion with Him, should be the cause of so much division among His followers, and that barriers should be erected round the Table of the Lord to prevent us all meeting together, all of us who name His Name as that of our Lord and Savior.

As I remarked about Bible-reading and prayer, so it is with the Holy Communion. There are many books written and easily available to suit every taste which will aid us in understanding this sacramental act, and in helping us the more worthily to partake. I want to stress three points only.

First, I think those of us who belong to one of the Reformed Churches should learn a lesson at this point from the Roman Church. There it is taught that to be absent wilfully from Mass on a Sunday morning is a mortal sin, that is, a sin which can produce deadly peril to the soul. I believe there is a genuine piece of spiritual truth being emphasized here, although I do not wish to press the point about *every* Sunday morning. In passing, however, I must refer to the New Testament suggestion that it was the practice of the early Christians to meet on each first day of the week for the breaking of bread. The point that matters, it seems to me, is the stress on the *regularity* of coming to the Holy Communion. We must not come just when we feel like it, or when we think we need some particular help. The great value of sacramental Communion is that it should be independent of our own subjective feelings, or our own personal needs. We come, in fellowship with others, to deepen our fellowship with our Lord by an outward and visible act—the receiving of the Sacrament. Experience shows that such a regular act does in fact maintain our communion with God, irrespective of our moods and feelings, of our ups and downs, of our sins and successes.

Another point worth making is this: The manner of the receiving of the Sacrament seems to me non-essential. In different communions we both celebrate and receive the Holy Communion in different ways. This is true; yet I myself find particular help in the fashion of the Anglican Church. Here we come up to the Table, kneel down in a line, and hold up our empty hands to receive the Sacrament of the Body and Blood of Christ. Notice the spirit of drama here. We are all levelled down as a whole group of sinners on our knees before Almighty God. This is an admirable reminder, always necessary when we seek to deepen our relationship with Him. There is no question of race or color, of intellect or understanding, of position or privilege, of goodness or badness; we are all needy, utterly needy sinners. We hold up our empty hands so that if the bread and wine are not placed into them, we go away empty-handed. This is another great reminder that we are utterly dependent in our relationship with God upon His love and upon His forgiveness. "Nothing in my hand I bring, Simply to thy cross I cling." "Unless thou save me I must die; O take me as I am." Here is a constant reminder of the great truth of justification by faith. I know that I am accepted, though wholly unacceptable. I know He receives me, not because of what I am, but because of what He is. My communion with Him does not rest upon my effort, or upon what I do, but upon His grace, and upon what He has done in Christ.

This is an authentic note of the Christian Gospel. It proclaims from the house-tops the essence of the Christian Faith, and makes clear beyond all shadow of doubt that the essential Christian experience of God is that of being accepted and forgiven by Him just as we are.

The third point to emphasize is the taking of the bread and eating it, the receiving of the wine and drinking it. Here is an act of identification, of appropriation, of making my own what is offered to me. What could stress more clearly the essential fact that unless Christ by His Spirit abides in me and I in Him, the fruits of the Christian life will never grow and develop? I am utterly dependent upon Him for the power to live for Him. Absolutely clearly it focuses upon my attention, and for that matter upon the attention of the world, that utter dependence upon God Himself is the essence of being a Christian.

There are, I fully recognize, many other facets that devout Christians see in the Eucharistic service, and devotional literature abounds with these insights. Yet these three simple points are quite sufficient to make it clear that together with Bible-reading and prayer this Sacrament is essential if the life of a Christian is to have within it the quality of genuine daily communion with his Master.

CHAPTER V

Christlikeness

I. EFFICIENCY

Tʜᴇ fourth mark or quality of the Christian life is that it is *a life of growth in Christlikeness*. We must "grow in grace, and in the knowledge of our Lord and Savior Jesus Christ."[1] "Christ . . . leaving us an example, that ye should follow his steps."[2] And as Paul puts it: "Be imitators of me, as I am of Christ."[3] John makes it crystal clear when he writes: "He who says he abides in him ought to walk in the same way in which he [Jesus] walked."[4]

What do we mean when we talk about Christlikeness? We make a mistake if we concentrate our meaning upon a literal imitation of Jesus. It is, of course, a very proper and sensible thing for a Christian to try to imitate the example of Jesus. It is an excellent challenge to ask ourselves from time to time, "What would Jesus do?"—yet at the same time we must bear in mind that from another point of view we cannot possibly literally imitate Jesus, for Jesus was unique. If the great Christian affirmation is true that the "Word became flesh," and that He "was made man," then the personality of Jesus is something and in some way different from ourselves. God has come and taken our human nature upon Him so that in that sense we can never imitate the unique God-Man that Christ was and is. Moreover, quite apart from His uniqueness Jesus

[1] 2 Peter 3:18
[2] 1 Peter 2:21
[3] 1 Corinthians 11:1 (*RSV*)
[4] 1 John 2:6 (*RSV*)

47

lived in a social environment utterly unlike that of the present day. Habits, customs, religious sanctions and moral standards were very different. All these make a slavish imitation of Jesus impracticable.

On the other hand, there is the possibility of imitation much in the same way as we can say of a young man: "He is the son of his father." We do not mean simply that he is the child of his father, or that in his veins the same life blood courses; we are suggesting that he has his father's likenesses, some of his father's characteristics—he is "a chip of the old block." In the same way Christ can be to us, perfectly properly, a standard, a guide to follow, an example.

By Christlikeness I want, however, to emphasize a rather different idea, as suggested by Paul: "And we all, with unveiled face, beholding the glory of the Lord, are being changed into his likeness from one degree of glory to another; for this comes from the Lord who is the Spirit."[5] "Unveiled face" refers to the fact that we can see God clearly in Christ, and can look upon Him without guilt and shame, because we are forgiven. Then Paul goes on to say that with this clear vision we can see something of the real nature and character of God—His "glory"— and that the result of this insight will be that we ourselves will be changed, so that in our turn in some small degree we shall become like Him, and shall reflect something of His own character and nature. Paul concludes: "This change is the work of the Holy Spirit."

Here, then, is the secret of Christlikeness. As we focus our thinking on Christ, so the Holy Spirit will begin to reproduce within us a little bit of the mind and temper of Jesus.[6] As the moon looks at the sun and so reflects the sun's likeness, I, if I look at Jesus, will find that by the Holy Spirit's help I shall be reflecting poorly but truly something of His likeness.[7]

Another analogy is worth considering. It is noticeable how sometimes two old people, a Darby and Joan, have grown to look like each other. As the years have passed during their

[5] 2 Corinthians 3:18 (RSV)
[6] Colossians 3:1,2
[7] Hebrews 12:2

married life they have been together so constantly, have looked at each other so frequently, that somehow they have grown very like each other, not only in ways and manners, but sometimes even in looks. If we have looked at Christ through the years, gradually perhaps some reflection of His ways and manners will be seen in us.

Yet here a warning note needs to be struck. We shall never notice this likeness in ourselves. The true Christian will never think that he is in the least Christlike, but if he is really allowing the Holy Spirit to work in his personality other people will occasionally notice in him a slight likeness to the Lord Jesus. That is really what Christlikeness means. It is not something that we can capture or achieve. We cannot make ourselves Christlike. If we possess it at all it is the Holy Spirit working out His ways in us; it is a fruit of the Spirit growing within us; it is the life of Christ reproducing within us something of His own character.[8]

What, then, are we endeavoring to do in our pursuit of Christian discipleship? Are we struggling to achieve this Christlikeness? Are we struggling to build a Christian character? Or are we letting the living Christ reproduce Himself in us? Are we, in the same way as we breathe the pure air into our lungs, allowing His Holy Spirit to fill us so as to bring forth His life in our lives? That is why though from one point of view there is struggle and effort involved in being a Christian, there is, on the other hand, the need to emphasize this idea of "letting go and letting God." It is as I face my real self, and accept God to be to me what He really is, that I shall discover increasing wholeness and integration. If I am part of the body of Christ, then I must allow the thought and impulses of the Head to flow through me, and to control my actions and to supply me with life.

> *Channels only, blessed Master,*
> *Yet with all thy wondrous power*
> *Flowing through us, thou canst use us*
> *Every day and every hour.*

[8] Philippians 2:3, Hebrews 13:21

This is what I really mean by Christlikeness, and in this sense we can speak of "the contemporary Christ." It is the Spirit of Christ alive and vital revealing Himself through His followers in every day and generation. If we would share in offering this revelation to the world our daily prayer might well be:

> Let the beauty of Jesus be seen in me,
> All His wonderful power and purity;
> O thou Spirit divine
> All my nature refine
> Till the beauty of Jesus be seen in me.

Having established this premise as to the meaning of Christlikeness, what follows? In passing we must notice that it is obviously a growth. No one can arrive at Christian maturity suddenly or quickly, but growth in the right direction there should and must be. Yet as with all growth we should not worry about it. Jesus Himself told us that we must not be over-anxious, for after all, anxiety will never add a cubit to our stature. I once heard of a young child who was trying to grow a bulb. Every day she uprooted it to see how it was getting on—and it didn't. So there are many Christian people who are introspective, always fretting about their progress and their spiritual growth; can they expect to grow naturally and steadily?

This gradual development within us of the temper and spirit of Jesus raises a tremendous subject. In what way will the Spirit of Jesus be seen? What are some of the likenesses we may expect? It is a fascinating and vast subject, and in this and the following two chapters I can select only six aspects for our consideration.

As I develop in Christlikeness it should mean a *rise in general personal efficiency*. It may seem surprising to headline this as the first aspect, yet I think it is important to do so. In the Gospels it is clear that Jesus was efficient in His daily work. He did all things well. As the village carpenter, although there is no Bible evidence for this, tradition suggests that He made good plows, good tables, and so on. He was a craftsman. When He made the five thousand sit down for the outdoor meal He made them sit, according to the meaning of the New Testament Greek word, in rows like a flower garden. It was well organized, it was a good party. The arrangements for the Last Supper went smoothly; His plan for His triumphal ride into Jerusalem worked without a hitch. As a story-teller He was magnificent, because He had an orderly mind, and marshalled His facts clearly and with imagination. Christians, if Christlike, should be efficient people. Paul saw this when he exhorted the Romans: "Don't be slothful in business"—in other words: Do your business properly.

This idea of efficiency reflecting the Spirit of Jesus must be applied not only to personal life, but also to the way in which Christians worship and conduct the business of the Church. I know it is possible to have an efficiently organized church which is not spiritual, but it should not be possible to have a spiritual church which is not efficient. Illustrations of what I mean abound.

The purpose of a hymn is to unite Christians in singing the praise of God—yet watch a congregation singing. So often there is little attempt to sing with enthusiasm and joy, so little attempt to bring out the meaning of the words, so little evidence that that united act of singing is an expression of united thoughts of praise and worship. This bad singing is plainly inefficient. Wesley's ideals for singing as expressed in the preface to the first collection of Methodist hymns strikes the right note: "The words should be worthy and full of Christian doctrine, and the tune should be dignified and singable, so that all may join in."

Two slight parentheses must be inserted here. Careless and casual hymn-singing is, of course, something much worse than inefficiency—inefficient though it is. It reveals a spiritual unreality in worship and ingratitude to God. Secondly, as an Anglican I must humbly acknowledge that Methodists as a general rule sing more enthusiastically than we do.

Another example is corporate prayer. The idea of saying "Amen" at the end of a prayer is to link the individuals in the congregation with the minister who has just spoken the prayer. The people's "Amen" is their agreement with what he has prayed. It is no sign of efficiency if at the end of a prayer instead of an audible and sincere "Amen" there is nothing but silence. I could mention many other points, such as punctuality in starting a service, the orderly movement of the service, and so on. Efficiency is no substitute for the worship of the heart; but worship of heart and mind should express itself in a well-ordered service.

This idea of efficiency should apply to the business administration of the Christian Church. We are beginning to realize that we can honor God by the stewardship of our money. Business organizations devoted to fund raising are often able to help congregations in educating themselves in the need for thoughtful and planned giving. What is surprising is the opposition encountered again and again by these organizations at meetings of church members. "The giving of money to God is a spiritual matter," it is objected. "There is no need to have a business organization to teach us how to do it. We don't want commercialism in the churches," and so on. These criticisms to my mind are not only invalid, but seem to miss the major point which I am making in this chapter. It is true that we shall never give to God a right proportion of our resources unless our hearts are filled with love and gratitude toward Him; but on the other hand efficiency is a Christian virtue. It is altogether proper and right that we should learn from experience how to be efficient both in raising and in spending the money for God's work.

In this connection it is distressing to hear on all sides how few members of most Christian congregations take the trouble to come to the business meetings of the church, and to be concerned with the management of its affairs. I write this with shame, for I suppose my own congregation at St. Martin's has some fifteen hundred members, and for our Annual Business Meeting we shall muster two hundred at the most. Here again I must admit that Methodist lay people take more interest in the business administration of their church than do Anglicans.

In personal life we shall never show the likeness of Christ as we should unless our daily lives are efficient. I remember once reading of a mother who attended a religious conference. She was greatly stirred, and longed to receive a special Blessing. This, according to the teaching she had heard, was the promise of a spiritual renewal, or the fullness of the Holy Spirit possessing her personality. Returning home, she spent extra time in studying her Bible, and prayed much longer each day than she had been doing. She was seeking for this Blessing. One day, after tea, she was reading her Bible and praying, looking for the coming of the Spirit, when her little girl of five ran up to her and said: "Mummy, please play with me. This is when you always do." "No, run away, darling," she replied; "Can't you see I am reading my Bible? I am seeking for a special Blessing from God." Disappointed and crestfallen the child answered: "Mummy, you are always reading your Bible nowadays, and you never play with me." That went straight to the mother's heart. Putting her Bible on one side, she played with her little girl, and as she played she found the Blessing, and felt a conviction that in some new way the power of God's Spirit was hers. As she sought to be an efficient mother so her Christian life deepened.

This is a very simple statement, but again and again it has been a tremendous help to those who have heard it. Busy housewives have been worried and anxious because they have so little time to read their Bibles, or to help in Church work. The feel they are being so little Christian in their witness and their work. Then they realize this great truth that being efficient in the house, making a real home of it, is in fact Christlike, and is a sign of genuine spiritual living. We must never try to separate the sacred from the secular. To the Christian everything is sacred, for everything is part of God's life, and is meant to be lived for Him. This world is God's world, and in seeking to make this world what it is meant to be we are doing God's business, and to do this efficiently is Christlike.

I am writing this chapter while staying in a Christian guest house, and it is a really Christian guest house, not because there is a great deal of corporate praying or other religious exercises—in fact, as a rule there are only fifteen minutes of simple family prayers in the morning and evening in the homely little chapel with its straw-covered floor. It is Christian because of the way it is run. The meals are simple and well cooked, and always punctual. The rooms are tidy, artistically decorated, spotlessly clean. Without haste or fuss the organization runs smoothly, and an atmosphere of peace pervades everything. The efficiency is there without being bustling or obtrusive. It is in this very basic sense a Christian guest house—very different from some which advertise themselves as such in the Church papers.

To the Christian business man the challenge comes to be more efficient in business, to the secretary to be more efficient as a secretary, to the friend to be a better friend. And I will add, since this book may well be read by young people, a student should become a better student. Sometimes one finds sixth-formers or university students neglecting their studies in order to help with religious meetings or Church activities. In reality their true Christian work is to pass their examinations.

There is a naturalness and rightness here which is very Christlike, and utterly devoid of "piousity." I heard of a young fellow who was a member of his trade union and a regular churchgoer. One Tuesday evening he turned up at a Bible study-group. His minister noticed him and said: "Tom, isn't tonight the night for the branch meeting of your trade union?" "Yes," he replied, "but tonight I thought I would come to the Bible study." "Nonsense," the minister retorted; "Go off to your branch meeting. That's the place where tonight you can serve God—being what you ought to be, an efficient member of your trade union."

That minister was quite right. One of the depressing facts of our modern industrial situation is that Christian men who work in our factories do not pull their weight in their branch activities. We owe a great deal in our Labor movement in Britain to the fact that many of its first leaders and pioneers were Methodist Local Preachers. Today things are very different, but it still is not too late for Christians of all denominations to see that one of their first duties is to be efficient in the activities of their particular trade union. I came across one such branch not long ago which had been dominated by three or four active Communists. Then three Christian men caught the vision of what their religion ought to mean, and began to go regularly to the meetings. At first it was boring; then as they began to speak out and take an active interest it became difficult —they were bullied; the Communists were rude to them; they were shouted down. They persevered, persuaded other men to come too and finally outvoted the Communists, and the branch became an efficient and truly representative branch. That was Christian action of a very Christlike kind.

I do not suggest that our society could be transformed by the multiplication of such actions, for the radical sin of human nature is deep and real, but it is indisputable that if Christians were really efficient in the business of daily life much of our present situation would be transformed. Far too many of us who call ourselves Christians believe we are better and more spiritual when we are praying than when we are working. The New Testament had no patience with such nonsense: "Whatever you do, in word or deed, do everything in the name of the Lord Jesus. . . . Whatever your task, work heartily, as serving the Lord."[9]

This challenge to Christlike efficiency will produce another very salutary effect. So often what prevents our efficiency are our sins. In business, for instance, there is prejudice against some new process or new idea. In international relationships we notice that an irrational antagonism toward or fear of rivalry from China or Russia prevents sound trade relationships. In personal life jealousy or a sense of shame hinders our actions. When we really see that Christ means us to be efficient in all spheres of our living then we shall seek to be freed by the power of God from these hampering sins which prevent us giving ourselves, and being our best.

[9] Colossians 3:17, 23 (RSV)

CHAPTER VI

Christlikeness

THE second aspect of the development of Christlikeness is a growth in the *real understanding of human nature*. Jesus understood men in a remarkable way. He understood them because He knew what was in them, and He gave a true value to human personality. As we become understanding Christians we reveal something of the Spirit of Christ. We shall do this not by reading psychology, although I think many Christians, especially ministers, would do well to study more than they do the ways in which the human mind works. We shall develop this understanding, however, as we allow the Spirit of Christ to work within us and we find ourselves possessing a deepened sympathy with others. We shall learn to be good listeners, and to do what the prophet Ezekiel did—we shall sit where they sit, put ourselves in the place of other people, and get alongside them, trying to understand them.

This should be so obvious as to be a mere platitude, but there are far too few Christians who are really conscientiously and continually seeking to get alongside others in sympathy and in listening. Quite often a young Christian married couple will ask me how they can best witness for Christ in their new home. There are plenty of avenues, of course, but I often question them about the friends they invite in to their house. I ask them how many friends they have in at once. The answer is "three or four," or something like that. They look surprised when I point out that perhaps that is two or three too many. I go on to say that one of the most helpful things a young couple can do is to invite just two others into their home, or even to have one friend in, and then one of the couple to slip into the kitchen so that two are left alone; or one to slip into the garden so that two can talk in the kitchen! Then there is a chance to listen, and to let the other talk.

Cardinal Newman understood this when he wrote: "How many souls are there in distress whose one need is to find a being to whom they can pour out their feelings unheard by the world. They want to tell them, and not to tell them; they wish to tell them to one who is strong enough to hear them, and yet not too strong so as to despise them." In this simple way of listening the young couple can make their home a place where their friends come to talk about themselves, to bring out their difficulties, and to open up their problems. In this sharing a Christian couple can have the opportunity of giving sympathy and understanding, offering their own experience, and in the end perhaps introducing their friends to Christ. This sounds so simple as I write it that I find myself wondering why thousands upon thousands more Christian people do not learn with God's help to give this very simple thing that anyone can give—a listening ear and a sympathetic mind.

We can examine this matter from another point of view. The New Testament makes it perfectly clear that part of a Christian's business is to help other Christians on in the Christian life. "Admonish the idle, encourage the faint-hearted, help the weak, be patient with them all."[1] The early Christian fellowship tried to do this when they confessed their faults one to another. The Methodist class-meetings were planned by Wesley for just this purpose. Today, however, in our modern Church life there is very little of this kind of activity. Certainly in the Anglican Church it is considered to be the business of the parson: the spiritual welfare of the congregation is his responsibility, and his alone. In the Presbyterian Church the elders are charged with this very duty, to assist the minister in spiritual and pastoral work. I am sure, however, if the truth were known, it is sometimes a matter of theory than of practice. The fact is that by and large, in Britain as in America, lay

[1] 1 Thessalonians 5:14 (RSV)

Christians are not nearly concerned enough with helping each other forward in Christian living. This failure makes little sense of Christian fellowship. As I pointed out recently to the young people in my own church: "You call yourselves Christians, but what have you done to help other Christians along? Your friends come to church; you worship together, you dance together, but do you ever help each other along in the Christian life? Perhaps you do by your influence and example, in fact I am sure you do, but do you go farther and try to help each other along by warning, by strengthening, by advising, by encouraging?"

This is a fair challenge by a minister to his own congregation. It is a still fairer challenge made by the people to the parson, for many of us who are parsons seem to be so busy that we forget that our first task is to look after the spiritual health of each member of our congregation.

If we are going to do this effectively, however, we must learn to understand human nature, and as I have already indicated, we shall learn to understand human nature by listening. We shall also learn the more faithfully we say our prayers, for the better we pray the more clearly we shall know God, and the more clearly we shall know ourselves, our real selves, and thus the more shall we know other people as they really are. I remember once a young seventeen-year-old public schoolboy saying to me: "Why is it that when you talk I feel so bad? You seem to hit me all the time, as if you know what I am thinking." "Because I know what I think and what I am," I replied, "I know what you think and what you are."

Another method that will help us to grow in a real understanding of human nature is if we try to see people as Christ saw people—realistically. He was never sentimental about people; He was always realistic. He saw people indeed as God's children, as God's sinful children. He saw much of the angel in man—the divine nature—but He also saw much of the devil —the self-centeredness that spoils. A well-known politician once said: "Human nature is essentially good." That was sentimentality. Jesus saw people as sinners needing forgiveness. Nehru was nearer to the facts of life when he told an

Indian friend of mine: "Before I came to power I stood for nationalization, and as much as possible. Now I am doubtful, because as far as I can see nationalization doesn't work unless people are either coerced or conscientious." That is most realistic. Man will work for the common good without incentive if he is coerced and forced to do so, or, on the other hand, if he is conscientious and really believes that co-operative living is the right way to live; but if he is neither conscientious nor coerced, then he will not work co-operatively, for self-interest steps in. Self-centeredness is the fly in the ointment. A growth in Christlikeness will give us increased understanding of men as they really are, and life as it truly is.

As our Christian understanding of human nature increases we begin to realize the possibilities of people. To use Paul's phrase, we shall see them as "brothers for whom Christ died." To put it another way, we shall begin to understand what is the Christian value of human personality. This is a real aspect of Christlikeness.

Some years ago, before the Second World War, a play entitled *The Mortal Storm* enjoyed a long run in London. Its theme centered on the Nazi régime, and its story concerned the break-up of a decent, happy, middle-class German family under the impact of the Nazi philosophy. The son, a young student, revealed the reason for the break-up when he said: "There is nothing above the State, nor beside the State. The individual is of no importance save as a servant of the State." There is plain atheistic philosophy. Man is no longer considered to be a child of God, with his own peculiar worth and value; he is just a unit to be used by the State—whatever that is—as it thinks fit. If a man is simply this and nothing more, if the State wishes to have some guinea pigs on which to try out some medical experiments and decides to light on the Jews, well, it doesn't matter—units have no rights, and have value only as they help the State. From this stemmed the vileness and beastliness of the treatment that individuals suffered. All powerful is the thing called the State (which on examination is a mere abstraction; it really stands for those who have power); in other words, some individuals treat the majority of individuals as mere things and units, giving to their personalities no real, intrinsic value at all. The majority are there to be used. In the same way in Communist philosophy the Party has the right to manipulate the masses for its own ends. This using of people for our own ends is the antithesis of the way that Jesus Christ saw individuals should be treated, for to Him each had a value of his own.

To be Christlike, then, we must seek to share the value that Jesus gave to human personality. What was it? In the first place, He believed that the human personality is meant to be a free personality—free to choose the ends of life, and to direct his action toward those ends. He was very particular to recognize this fact about men. He always treated people as having free will and the right to choose. This does not, of course, imply complete free will to do what I like. I live within society—a society of other free souls. You have no right to say to me: "I choose to throw my rubbish over your back-garden wall." My reply is clear: "Thank you. I don't want it." Your will may be free, but so is mine. There are, therefore, limits within a free society to an individual's free will. We have to live in community. There is a common good as well as an individual good. But within these limits Christ placed a tremendous emphasis on the right, and indeed on the need, of a man to be free. In His eyes it was God's will that I should live and develop as a free-choosing personality. That is why He rejected the subtle temptation of the devil when he was standing on the platform of the Temple. He refused the suggestion to come floating down miraculously from the platform so that everybody would be overwhelmed by the wonder of it, and would be magnetized into believing in Him. He had no intention of dominating man's mind, of sweeping him off his feet by some emotion, of brain-washing him. Our Lord's approach to the individual was to offer him truth, to offer him love. If truth was rejected, if love was refused, then He was content to be rejected and crucified. Christ lived and died to establish this understanding of the value of human personality.

If we seek to become Christlike, we, too, have in practical daily life to stand for this value for the individual. What does this mean in practice? It means, for instance, that we must reject the possessiveness of power. We have no right to use undue and unfair influence over others for our own advantage and to further our plans. Parents must not be possessive of their children, but must be willing to allow their children to develop their own independence, to learn by their own experience, to make their own mistakes. We have no right to try to mould them to be like us, or to expect them to live the kind of life we would like them to live. We can offer them our best experience, give them our love, put before them the ways of goodness and truth—but then they must make their own choice.

It means, too, that generally speaking a Christian cannot be a revolutionary and support unconstitutional action backed by force. He must stand for the gradualism of persuasion.[2] Logically this will mean that Christians cannot contract out of political action, and that whether we like it or not we must play our part in the party politics of today even if it means only taking a thoughtful and responsible action when we vote. For some it may mean at a great deal of sacrifice "going into politics." One of the rather dismal features of today's life is to observe that both in national and local politics some of the best men of all parties refrain from standing for the local council or for Parliament. It may well be a Christlike action to do just this work and to do it because only in this way within the democratic structure can real freedom be maintained.

From another point of view this element of Christlikeness asserts the right of free speech, and the need to tell the truth and to reveal the facts. We can never agree to liquidating opponents, to the suppression of facts by the Government, or by anyone else, to misrepresentation by the Press, and mass propaganda. People must be allowed to know the truth, and then to decide. It seems to me quite unchristian when Church people work up an agitation to keep agnostics off the television screen. I do not agree with their agnostic views, but as a

[2] This is generally true notwithstanding Bonhoeffer's agonized acceptance of a part in the Hitler plot, or the Presbyterian theology of tyrannicide, etc.

Christian I believe they have a right to be heard and to be seen.

In business this idea means that as an employer I should try to explain as many facts as I can to the employees in my industry. They have a right to be told what is happening, and to be invited to contribute their thoughts to dealing with the situation. Christlikeness at this point is a very searching thing. It hits right against our love of power, and this love of power is one of the most menacing features of this age. We are moving into what has been called by Dr. James Burnham an era of managerial revolution. In industry the managerial class is all powerful; in government it is the managerial bureaucrat; in social life the managerial technician or welfare officer. All these trends minister to man's love of power to dominate. Christlikeness would lead us, while accepting the need for change in this age of technology, to be on our guard against this temptation, and to fight it wherever it rears its ugly head. Today the battle is joined against economic and mental slavery as truly as it used to be against physical slavery.

All this may sound somewhat platitudinous, but if we search our own hearts and minds we cannot fail to see that the infection of the disease of love of power has in some way affected all of us, and that the remedy here is to allow the Spirit of Christ to heal and to strengthen us.

In the second place, Jesus saw the value of human personality not only in being a free-choosing being, but in the uniqueness of each individual. A man is of distinctive value and worth to God. We can remember how Jesus referred to the *one* lost son, the *one* lost sheep, the *one* lost coin, as mattering tremendously to the owner. Each was unique, and of its own particular worth. We may have our physical doubles in some part of the world, but there can never be a personality double. Each of us with all his own personal experience is himself, and God loves him as he is, for He has no favorites. I remember a small girl asking me once: "How can God love everybody at once?" Any good mother with a large family could answer that. In an amazing way she can love her family as a whole, each individual specially, and everyone equally. The more she loves, the more she can love. God's infinite love can embrace all of us, and yet love me individually and in a special way.

It follows that if I am loved by God in this way, and have unique worth, then so has every other individual. Growth in Christlikeness will enable me to recognize the infinite worth of each person as a person. There can never be any "herrenfolk" with a right to dominate others because they are of more worth. We cannot accept the idea held by some who call themselves Christians in South Africa that God predestined some people to hew wood and draw water, and so to serve the white man. The hymn is unchristian that says, "The rich man in his castle, the poor man at his gate," suggesting as it does that both are meant to stay where they are.

It is interesting to notice that when Jesus linked two commandments of the Old Testament together—"Thou shalt love the Lord thy God with all thy heart" and "Thou shalt love thy neighbor as thyself"—he made clear two facts. First, that because God loves me in a true and personal way I should love Him back in return; and second, that I must love my neighbor whom God also loves, but I need not love him better than myself, but *as* myself. It is true that if I really respect myself, and believe that I am loved by God as an individual, it should follow that I should recognize that other individuals are my equals and I should treat them so.

This idea of equal worth and value does not lead us into the ridiculous idea that everyone has equal aptitudes, and that, therefore, all of us, for instance, ought to have equal pay, or equal this and that. The facts of life show this to be nonsense. It does mean, however, that we cannot exploit individuals, for they are God's loved persons. We must not exploit them for fun, for expediency, for business, for politics. It means, too, that we must work to obtain for each of God's children equality of opportunity, and that as rising standards of human living are possible they are made available for all to enjoy.

We must recognize, however, that at any given point of history there will be certain differences, many inequalities, and some social separateness. There will be the under-privileged groups and the more privileged groups. Christlikeness in outlook will prompt us to work to remove this wrongness from human society, and to allow individuals to move freely from one group to another as they seize the opportunities they are offered. Repression and refusal to give equality of opportunity are sins.

Put like this in face of the world situation today the task looks gigantic and impossible. So it must have looked to the first Christians, a tiny minority in a pagan world. They sought first in the community of the Church to mirror what the Christ-like life should be. As Paul grandly put it: "There is neither Greek nor Jew, circumcision nor uncircumcision, Barbarian, Scythian, bond nor free: but Christ is all, and in all."[3] I think it may well have been this real family spirit, this genuine fellowship, this deep and living sense that within the Christian community each was loved for himself and regarded as of equal worth, that attracted the outsiders toward Christianity. Women and children, rich and poor, clever and ignorant, good and bad, all were alike welcome.

Today, unfortunately, it still happens that the Christian Church can be a place of snobbery and class distinction. Money and reputation can still pull strings, and count for more than they ought within the life of the organized Church. The truth of this charge does not need to be proved. It is, unfortunately, open and apparent to all who know the life within all denominations. Here is a sin which Christians could deal with if they would; and if they did, they would enable the Church to bear a most attractive witness to the world outside, for power, position, money still count and mitigate against the true equality of man.

I well remember when I was Vicar in a West End parish in London one of the wealthiest ladies in my congregation coming to see me. She found fault with me—perhaps quite fairly—for all that I was trying to do for the young people who were starting to come to church. She complained that I was altering the services, and not using the Prayer Book fully. She preferred her Prayer Book services exactly as written, and de-

[3] Colossians 3:11

manded that I should have them so. I apologized and explained that some variation and adaptation was necessary if the young people were to be drawn into the Church and helped forward in their Christian lives. Her reply was unrelenting: "I don't mind about the young people, whether they are helped or not. I like my own church as it always has been." "But, Madam," I answered, "you will soon be dead; and when you are, there will be no Church if the young people are not built up in the Body of Christ." "Very well, then," she retorted, "I shall leave your church and withdraw my subscriptions." This she did; but the story has a happy ending. Six months later she came back, and because at heart she was a grand old lady, she sought me out and told me: "That other church was too dull, so I have come back to you." She was a faithful member for another two or three years, and gave me a measure of her friendship until she passed on, a good Christian soul, into the fuller life.

She had got the wrong idea. She thought her money made a difference—it gave her position and influence, and therefore she had the right to call the tune within the Church of God. These distinctions must disappear from our thinking and our acting if we are to show any likeness to our Master.

In the third place Jesus recognized that if the true value of human personality is to be seen the individual must be treated as, and be able to live as, a responsible being. He showed this clearly in His story about the talents. What mattered was not how many talents a man had, but did he use the talents he possessed? In other words, a man cannot live as a true child of God unless he is working creatively with his talents upon the stuff of life. The socialist phrase, "To each according to his need, and from each according to his ability," is basically true in its Christian idealism. We are suffering today from the selfish demand from individuals that each of them should receive not only according to need, but according to desire, and at the same time a refusal to give to the community according to ability. This decay of a sense of responsibility for being creative is sapping at the very foundations of modern life. Everywhere it is apparent; and what ought not to be surprising is that it is also becoming apparent that the world will not work this way, that life cannot be lived with a refusal of responsibility. Wealth—true wealth, which is the working upon natural resources for the welfare of mankind—cannot be produced without creativeness and the acceptance of individual responsibility for taking a share in the work. Yet blindly we stagger along, selfishly seeking to get rather than to give. It is no wonder that this modern civilization in such conditions creates strain and tension, stomach ulcers and neuroses. We are just not being our true selves.

Admittedly this is not altogether the fault of individual men and women. We have moved into the machine age, and machines tend to destroy creativeness and craftsmanship. They take away from the meaningfulness of daily work. Many people in our large industrial cities "Go to work to earn the cash to buy the bread to get the strength to go to work to earn the cash to buy the bread . . . , etc."—a kind of treadmill existence. There is no interest in their work, and it is largely repetitive.

I know, of course, that many operatives like this kind of labor. They find that as they do it automatically their mind can think of other things; they can dream dreams; they can talk to each other; but—and there is no escaping from this—they find no creative outlet in what they are doing as their daily work. For eight hours every day they are not acting as creative, responsible people. Automation will produce even more of this kind of work as it invades larger areas of industry. What can be done? We cannot get rid of machines, as I think Eric Gill suggested; yet something must be done.

In this connection I remember some twenty-seven years ago that visionary and prophet, Canon C. E. Raven, saying in a sermon that leisure and the right use of leisure would be the problem for the latter half of this century. That he is right is beyond argument, but I wish I could feel that we were showing any success in helping the mass of the people to be creative in their leisure hours, and to live as responsible people. We seem to be floundering in a mass of inertia, realizing that we are sinking, but not knowing how to get out.

There would be some hope on the horizon if there were signs that we were acting responsibly in the one sphere where machines can never prevent us from being creative, that is in the sphere of personal relationships; but is there any sign of this responsible action—within the personal relationship of family life, between the different groups in society, between management and labor, between ourselves, and between the nations? In all these there seems little that is creative, and much that is irresponsible.

In these three aspects in which Christ underlined the value of human personality there is plenty of scope for action for Christians who seek in any measure to show within themselves the Spirit of Christ. If Christians are seeking for action, then action is surely open to them along countless avenues in everyday life.

CHAPTER VII

Christlikeness

III. WILLINGNESS TO SUFFER

A THIRD aspect of Christlikeness is *the willingness to suffer.* The New Testament is full of references to the suffering and sacrifice a Christian must be willing to face if he is to follow his Master. Paul writes that he is glad to share in the fellowship of His sufferings,[1] and goes on to point out that only if we are willing to suffer with Him shall we share in His triumph.[2] Part of the Christian experience is not only to receive the gift of faith, but to be called to accept sacrifice[3]—in fact, Paul could describe his experience in these words: "I am crucified with Christ: nevertheless I live."[4]

In the gospel story there is that delightful incident when the wise men came bringing their gifts to the infant Christ. Kneeling before Him, they opened their treasures and presented unto Him gifts—"gold, and frankincense, and myrrh."[5] We are not being over-fanciful if we take these gifts as symbols of our offering to Christ, our King. He wants the truly valuable gold of our personalities yielded to Him; the daily frankincense of our prayer and worship must ascend to His throne; and then there is the myrrh. Myrrh typifies suffering and death, and part of the dedication of the Christian is the offering to God of our dying to self, and our willingness to suffer.

Christ specifically called us to this idea of sacrifice. "If any

[1] Philippians 3:10, 2 Corinthians 1:7
[2] Romans 8:17, 2 Timothy 1:7, 12
[3] Philippians 1:29
[4] Galatians 2:20
[5] Matthew 2:11

man will come after me, let him deny himself, and take up his cross daily, and follow me. For whosoever will save his life shall lose it: but whosoever will lose his life for my sake, the same shall save it."[6] Canon Streeter paraphrases this saying of our Lord thus: "If you think to be one of my disciples you must say 'no' to self, and remember that you are living with a halter round your neck." A mark of Christlikeness then is to live with a halter round one's neck. What does this mean, to live always wearing a symbol of death?

It is important first of all to clear out of the way any ideas of a false asceticism. There is no suggestion in the teaching of the New Testament that we are to seek suffering for suffering's sake, or to practise self-denial simply for the sake of saying no. The conception that God values the mutilation of the body, or the crushing of ordinary human desires, is pagan, and not Christian. Christ's religion is not a negation of life; it is the discovery of positive, real, eternal living.

Christian self-denial, then, is not practised by creating a list of taboos, fastings and abstentions. We shall not achieve it by refusing to eat meat on Fridays, or by abstaining from dancing or the theatre. Shutting ourselves off from the world in a monastery or convent, or leaving all the friends we love and rushing to darkest Africa are not in themselves necessarily the carrying out of our Lord's command to say "no" to self and bear His Cross. The essence of Christian self-denial is when I seek to substitute His will for my will; to say "no" to myself in order to say "yes" to Him. There is something of active response and of glad acceptance in the spirit of the Christian who denies himself. Perhaps it is clearer if we think of the "saying 'no' to self" as being a preliminary to taking up the Cross, much as repentance is the gateway to faith. Dropping that which may hinder, I can grasp at that which is good.

There is a misunderstanding, too, in many people's minds about the Cross we have to carry in Christ's name. So often in pastoral work I come across, for instance, an old woman who tells me that with patience she is trying to bear her cross;

[6] Luke 9:23

this turns out to be some illness, or the loss of some dear relative. But our Lord is not referring, in His challenge, to this kind of cross, for the pains and sorrows of life are not a cross we can take up or refuse to take up; they come upon us and hit us whether we choose them or not. They are part of the stuff of life in which we Christians have to live; we can neither accept them nor reject them. They have to be met when they come.[7] Our Lord was inviting us in His name and for His sake to take up a cross, and implies that we can either take it up or refuse it. To what is He referring?

He means, I am sure, a deliberate saying "no" to self, and the deliberate acceptance of the willingness to suffer in some particular way for a particular purpose so that we may carry out His will and further His kingdom.

Before we examine the implication of this more fully it is worth while noting in passing that this element of self-denial and suffering introduces into the Christian experience what I should like to call an element of iron or steel. So much Christian living is flabby, soft and comfortable. There is no real sacrifice involved, no real hardness to be endured. Many who read these words will, like myself, be neither Roman Catholics nor puritan Evangelicals. We specially need to heed this challenge of our Lord. In their own way Roman Catholics have an element of iron in their religion. Their rules of fasting, the need for regularity at Mass, the obligation of regular confession, the fear of hell, and the absolute authority of the Church over body and soul—here indeed are disciplines enough, and much sacrifice is demanded to respond as one ought in sincerity and truth. Alas, many Roman Catholics are never able so to respond.

The Puritan Evangelical feels that many things are wrong for him which others can enjoy. The list varies, but often includes dancing, cards, the theatre, films, and so on. We should never ridicule a young Christian who for His Lord's sake turns his back upon the natural and good things of life. In so doing he expresses the depth of his love for his Lord, and there is a .

---

[7] But perhaps facing an illness courageously and serenely for Christ's sake may deserve the title "bearing the cross."

real element of iron in his religious faith. The danger for him lies in a later reaction when he may find that he has been renouncing things that need not be renounced, and clinging to things which he should have yielded.

Those of us, however, who pride ourselves that we are free from these narrow restrictions, and from what we regard as man-made restraints, must face with the utmost sincerity this demand of our Lord, otherwise there will not be the steel in our living which is part of being a Christian.

Examining the matter more closely we first have to face the suffering involved in a definite allegiance to Christ. Secret discipleship is not really possible. If I am to witness for Christ I must do it in the open, and that is where the suffering begins. In its stark nakedness we can see it more easily in other lands than our own. It is still true in an Islamic country that to be a Christian, and a baptized Christian, may cost a man his life. It will certainly involve social ostracism and utter loneliness. For an orthodox Jew to become a Christian will mean the rending of what to a Jew are the closest of all ties, the ties that bind him and his family together.

Some years ago there came to Birmingham Parish Church a young Hindu. His father was a lay Hindu high priest in Assam, wealthy and aristocratic. The young fellow came to our church because an older brother had told him: "When you go to England go along to a Christian Church. You will find the people there sociable and friendly, but they will not try to make you a Christian, so you need not worry." He found with us, so he told me after a time, friendship and kindness; he was accepted by our young people, and made to feel at home. Two or three years passed. He prayed with us, and he worshipped with us. Some of our young people discussed religion with him, but nobody tried to convert him. Then the Gospel of Christ began to work in his heart and mind. At length he made his decision and accepted Christ as his Savior and Lord. He came and asked me for baptism. "I can never return to my father's home, I know; it might even mean death if I did. As well as this exile I am willing to suffer anything in gratitude for the love of Christ." One Whit Sunday morning I baptized him. As I did so, more vividly than before I understood something of the meaning of the suffering of allegiance.

This suffering may be seen more vividly in other lands, but exists most really in Britain today. Many a man working in a factory has to face ridicule when after a weekend he admits that he has been to church, and gets the reputation of being a practising Christian. The suffering is very real. It has nothing to do with being ashamed of naming the name of Christ. Most Christians are not ashamed of Him in the least—far from it. The hurt lies in being different, a sense of loneliness and estrangement from one's fellows. We hate the thought that they may believe that we think we are better than they are —if our friends are good, decent living people, we hate this. Yet we are different; we are living with a different purpose, we hope to live in a different spirit. We are with them, yet not of them. This is a very real mental and spiritual suffering.

This is particularly true and painful when it occurs within one's own family. In most Christian congregations today there are people of all ages who are the only members of their family to attend church, the only ones who profess to be Christian. Here is intense loneliness, for of all places where we hope to be understood, and want to be our natural selves without strain and stress, it is in our homes, but if one is the only Christian there that is not possible. We have to be on our guard; we do not want to let Christ down; we do not want to be misunderstood.

Jesus knew something of this from His own experience. His mother and His brethren did not understand Him, and that hurt. He shared with us His experience when He said: "Think not that I am come to send peace on earth: I came not to send peace, but a sword. For I am come to set a man at variance against his father, and the daughter against her mother, and the daughter in law against her mother in law. And a man's foes shall be they of his own household."[8]

Willingness to suffer must also show itself in the active acceptance of self-discipline. In a later chapter I shall try to show

[8] Matthew 10:34

that the Christian life is a life of freedom, and that it is not
bound by rules and regulations. This is true; but there is still
a call to self-discipline. There may be no rules imposed from
outside, but we must impose them on ourselves. Paul makes
this point when he tells us: "I keep under my body, and bring
it into subjection."[9]

It is a wise habit for a Christian to frame for himself some
simple rule of life. For instance, the length of time that we
spend on saying our daily prayers does not matter, but the rule
to say them does. The frequency of attendance at the Holy
Communion is not the main point; but the regularity is. The
way of reading the Bible in private devotion can be varied; but
the habit should be fixed. It is here that young Christians often
need help, and in many Church guilds there is the practice
of suggesting that each member should draw up his own rule
of life after thought and prayer, and also, if necessary, after a
quiet discussion with the minister, or some older Christian
friend. However it is done, a simple rule is a good safeguard
against becoming casual in spiritual exercises.

This idea of self-discipline, however, has wider implications.
It embraces the control of my thoughts. Let me say at once I
am not referring to training myself to abstain from thinking un-
kind, impure and other wrong thoughts; what I am suggesting
is the need to find the discipline of concentration whereby
I can keep my mind from wandering or from day-dreaming,
and can fix it upon matters that need my attention. Frequently
I am asked by some earnest Christian for help in concentrating
during prayer time. I commonly begin by asking: "Can you
concentrate at other times?" This learning of thought-control
is important not only to our devotions, but to our daily living.

We need self-discipline, too, over our feelings. Some of us
are too prodigal with them, and let them run away with us.
We are moody, or we are passionate, but we are certainly not
controlled.

Then there is our will. Hasty and impulsive action has
ruined many a Christian's witness; retracing our steps is a hard

[9] I Corinthians 9:27

and difficult business when we have acted wrongly. That is why it often helps to obtain discipline of will if we will practise doing something or not doing something which in itself is of no importance. The exercise of will in such a matter can help us to find the discipline we seek. It is said that John Wesley's mother made a practice of training her children's wills, so that they learnt this discipline. It is a valuable training.

There is, too, the willingness to suffer in the active acceptance of limitation. One of the amazing things about the Incarnation is the phrase of Paul's: "He emptied himself."[10] What exactly this emptying or *kenosis* means has been the subject of endless debate among Christian scholars, but whatever it means, it shows the amazing self-limitation of God, His willingness to limit Himself that He might become one with us. The Christian in his turn has to be willing to accept this limitation and do so gladly.

I remember once reading the story of a wonderful priest who had given the best years of his life working amid terrible conditions in the east end of London. One day he returned to his Oxford college for a reunion with friends of his student days. He sat drinking coffee with two of his particular friends. They talked of their travels, of the countries they had seen, the picture galleries they had visited, and the music they had heard. The priest sat silent. He, too, was a cultured man, and he loved all these things of beauty; he, too, would have liked to have travelled, but he had had no time. He had been busy amongst his poor and suffering people; besides, he had no money. As he listened a shadow of wistfulness passed across his face. He felt limited; his capabilities could have reached so much farther; but even as the shadow fell across his face there were scores of people in his East End parish who thanked God for him, and that he had been willing to suffer that limitation.

In some measure this challenge comes to every Christian. We have only so much energy, time, ability, and so on. If we are going to serve Christ, and for His sake to serve our fellow

[10] Philippians 2:7 (RSV)

men, then some other things must go, and be laid on one side. It is difficult for a Christian to be a millionaire; not that for one moment am I suggesting that it is wrong to have money, if we use it wisely as a trust of which we are stewards. It is rather that money-making, if that is to be the great purpose of our lives, will hardly be possible if we are to find time and energy to serve Christ, and others for His sake. There may well be a call here to limit some activities for the sake of other and more worth-while activities.

This same thought of limitation may guide a young science student who could almost certainly earn a large salary in industry, but who because the need is greater, deliberately takes up the vocation of teaching. It might come to a scholar who could be a Fellow of his college, and enjoy the facilities of research and teaching in his own country, but who for the service of Christ goes out to Africa to teach in a theological college future African priests.

When I was in Ghana it was sad to meet a number of lecturers in the University there who seemed to me to be missing the point of vocation. Some of them would, no doubt, call themselves professing Christians, but it appeared that they were there largely for self-interest. The conditions of work and the salaries in the University were good; there was ample opportunity for them to complete their London University doctorates. They did their teaching no doubt adequately, but they showed little interest in their students. In the judgement of myself and others they were there for their own purposes, and not to serve the students in Ghana.

There were, of course, exceptions. Amongst these were a young married couple, both lecturing in different faculties. As Christians they had chosen to go to Ghana. Their home was open to the students, and they tried to identify themselves with their interests. This involved, to some extent, a limitation of their own interests, and certainly took up a good deal of their leisure time from their own work and social pleasure, but in accepting this limitation they were giving to those African students something utterly and completely worth while.

This acceptance of limitation often means that in love for

God and our fellow men we are willing to accept that which is to us, from a natural and temperamental point of view, unpleasant and undesirable. I remember in Rhodesia meeting a young and cultured woman, vivacious and full of fun, who deliberately chose to visit lonely old ladies that she might talk with them and read to them. As she put it: "I know it cheers them up, but I must admit I often find it boring." Of course she found it boring; that was natural, but she deliberately decided to accept this that she might serve.

On that same visit a Government official was converted to Christ. He consulted me about his future. Opening his heart, he told me of the grave restrictions put upon him by the Government policy toward the Africans. He felt that now in the light of his Christian experience many things he would have to do according to the law would be repugnant to him. "Shall I quit," he asked me, "and find another job, or shall I stay where I am? Probably next year I shall become head of my department of native affairs. Then, though obviously I cannot alter the law, I can administer it in as humane and Christian a way as possible." I did not advise him; we merely talked and prayed together, but I must confess I was glad when he told me later that he was going to stay where he was, accepting the limitation of a difficult position for Christ's sake.

Another form of self-limitation is linked with Church membership. This may sound surprising, but it is true. In England, unlike America, it is not the conventional or done thing to be a regular church attender. A man who genuinely links himself with some branch of the Christian Church and regularly attends its local meeting-place is to some extent a marked man. His Church membership makes demands upon him which to some extent will limit his leisure time, and his energy for other pursuits. To be a real member of the Christian Church calls for the acceptance of the responsibility of belonging. This involves not merely regular Church worship, but a willingness, for instance, to offer one's expert professional services to look after the business of the local church, to become a vestryman or a deacon, to take up visiting; it may perhaps call upon a man to volunteer to help in a youth club, or to take a Sunday-school class—this latter is a wonderful privilege that calls for time for preparation as well as for teaching. In the Parish Church at Gerrards Cross there is a most flourishing Children's Church, and there a good number of fathers who were but loosely attached at the beginning now gladly share the duties of leading that Children's Church, or helping in some other way. This may limit their time in the garden or for playing golf, but it is quite certainly an acceptance of Christian responsibility. A responsibility such as this we are all tempted to evade especially if we are successful business men, yet it must not be evaded, just as the responsibility of parenthood must not be evaded.

A headmistress of my acquaintance told me recently about a difficult adolescent girl in her school. She was insubordinate, disobedient, lazy and thoroughly wild. After many attempts the headmistress finally talked the matter over with the parents. Her father said: "I agree, something must be done. Will you please thrash her for me?" Quite apart from the advisability of corporal punishment, here was a plain evasion of fatherhood! Many Christians are quite willing to let other people run the Church family while they sit back and avoid the limitation of their time and energy which such a responsibility involves.

In the modern complex world of industry and business a Christian has to face the possibility of limiting his acquiring of money. The Bible nowhere suggests that to have money is wrong. What is sinful is when money "has" us, or, as the Bible describes it, the "love of money." This implies that the Christian has to turn his back resolutely upon doubtful ways of gaining easy money. This is obvious, but what is not so obvious and is infinitely more difficult is to see when it is necessary to decide to make a stand and to refuse to compromise, though it may involve a financial loss. No one can tell any other to do this, but we need to ask for a sensitive conscience to discern it for ourselves.

One of the finest men in my congregation was faced with this situation. A newly elected director and secretary of a company, he found that under Government restrictions his firm was engaging in both illegal and non-moral practices. He protested, but any protest he made was of no avail. Finally he said he would resign and leave, if a change was not made. He had to leave. As a married man with two children this was a real sacrifice, for after much searching the only post he could get for which his qualifications fitted him was one with about half the salary.

This principle applies not only to a fairly clear case such as this, but also to matters concerning the choice of a house, the possession of television, the purchase of an expensive car. Clearly these things are legitimate for a Christian to acquire, but there is need to face the expenditure of our money on what is not absolutely essential. How far has the Christian the right to spend freely on himself and his family, when the cause of God needs financing, and the world is full of those living just on starvation line? There is no easy answer here, but there does seem to be room for us to face, for the sake of Christ, limitation that we may better serve the cause of our Master.

In all these examples the emphasis is not on limitation for limitation's sake, but on the willingness to be limited that we may be free fully to follow the way of Christ's service.

There is also the willingness to suffer in the active acceptance of alteration. In the same way as the Christian life is not static, but progressive, so Christian thought must never be static, but must always progress. When Jesus told us to love God He said that we had to love Him with all our mind, as well as with all our heart, and it is far too easy to get too fixed in our habits of thinking and acting. Jesus must have startled his contemporaries with His vivid ways of communication, and by His unorthodox methods of approach. New wine must be put into new wine skins, He told His disciples.

The Christian message is the age-old Gospel, but it needs to be expressed in new thought-forms, and in new methods, with each generation. We have only to study the New Testament to see how the writers of the different books struggled to use the word-pictures and thought-forms of their age, that through them they might be able adequately and clearly to bring the Gospel home to their hearers. The same demand is made upon the Christian Church in this generation, whether it be in Africa and Asia or here in Europe.

It has been interesting to notice recently some of the television programs in which scientific humanists such as Julian Huxley and Margaret Knight have been suggesting that humanism is sufficient to enrich the human experience and to save mankind, without any belief in God being necessary; morals are possible without religion. Paradise can be regained without faith. In these discussions I have observed that often the Christian protagonists do not seem able to reach the heart of the humanist argument. They make assertions and philosophical statements which had point and validity some decades ago, but do not seem logical nor relevant to the modern humanist. I cannot help wondering whether the Christian apologist of middle age has failed to move with the times in his thinking, so that his arguments are geared to another and earlier age.

I sometimes think that this is partly true in the theological colleges of all the Churches. I wonder whether the way in which Christian doctrine is expounded and taught is really relevant to the climate of opposition and argument the minister of religion meets in the real world outside. I know that we cannot argue people into belief in God, but none the less it does become necessary that the Christian religion should make sense to thoughtful people. The mass of knowledge that they have acquired in other fields should not seem to have to be put in one water-tight compartment while their Christian faith and experience is put into another; rather it should be that within the whole range of their culture and knowledge the Christian faith in God should seem to make sense of the whole. To achieve this outlook we need to be willing to suffer the alteration of our ideas; and to some extent this is always painful. We like to cling to what we have always believed; we are afraid to face the struggle of doubt or the disturbance of questioning, so we refuse to alter our ideas or to broaden our thinking.

The same dislike of alteration applies to the changing of habits whether of worship or of practice. Examples leap to one's mind—where middle-aged church-goers have resisted suggestions of new methods, or where parents have insisted that their children should follow the habits of conduct and conventions of their own childhood. Fixity of habit can certainly have a stabilizing effect, and it is a good thing that after adolescence most of us settle down to regular lives based on accepted habits and ways of thought; but even in this stability there can be danger; we can refuse to face the need for alteration, to see a better and newer way, and to pursue it. One of the most heartening experiences is to meet some old person, a woman of deep saintliness and of active mind; as one talks with her one discovers that in spite of her age her mind is alert and eager; she welcomes and rejoices in new ways and new ideas; she doesn't accept them easily, for she has a long and solid experience of the past to guide her, but she is willing to see and to embrace that which is new, if it is really good and valuable. Here is a picture of what the Christian Church should ever be—drawing on the wisdom of the past, but willing to suffer the need of continual alteration.

The Christian must also be willing gladly to accept the suffering of pain and ultimate death. In themselves pain and disease are evil. The full range of the healing power of God extends not only to the healing of the soul from sin, but to the healing of the body from disease; but as long as we live in the body, so long we are liable not only to temptation and sin, but also to pain and physical illness. When this meets us, the Christian attitude is not one of fatalism and resignation; it should be one of glad resolve that in and through the pain there shall be glory to God, and the learning of some lesson otherwise impossible to be learnt. Someone has said that here is the garden where God's best flowers can grow.

I remember talking some years ago to a very brilliant surgeon. For two years, through a finger cut and poisoned during an operation, she had suffered intense agony and pain. On several occasions her life had been despaired of, but now at last she had recovered. Simply and without melodrama she remarked: "I would not have missed this experience of pain for anything. In it the presence of Christ has been more real than ever before."

In his striking book, *Determined to Live,* my friend, Brian Hession, reveals the same kind of acceptance. Given three days to live because of cancer of the rectum he tape-recorded his thoughts about his approaching death. After a surprisingly successful operation his life was saved, and he picked up his work again. For three years now he has moved about the world lecturing and speaking about the power of faith to help people to conquer the fear of pain and disease. Thousands must be grateful to him for his ministry—a ministry only possible because he himself was willing to accept pain and death.

The same characteristic is to be seen in that remarkable book, *Margaret,* where a young girl of sixteen was told she was dying of cancer. As she slowly became worse, she accepted it with faith and courage and a complete trust in the love of God; and thus her last months were a witness to all who came to her bedside. They found in her the God whom they were seeking for themselves, and quite a number were brought into a living experience of Christ. After all, Easter Day was only possible because Christ moved through Gethsemane to Golgotha.

Lastly, there is the willingness to care for people; and such real caring must always cause suffering. We cannot care without being hurt ourselves. Jesus, when He saw the city, wept over it.

The Bible calls Christians by different names, but one rather beautiful description is that we are "a royal priesthood." What then is a priest? The writer of the Epistle to the Hebrews describes him as one who "stands on the godward side" of the world, showing that a true priest must firstly be God-appointed, and secondly one of ourselves. Thus only can he stand between us and God. The Christian, as it were, is placed in the middle as a mediator, even as Christ in a unique sense was the "one mediator between God and man." As His master did, so the individual Christian must make it his business—the Father's business—to lift up the world to

God in prayer on the one hand, and then on the other to take the Word of God as he knows it for himself, and to offer it to the world that needs to know it. He stands on the godward side.

This is a position, however, of suffering, because we cannot really pray for people unless we are close enough to them to know their real needs, and these real needs, if we are sensitive, must hurt us. We cannot offer the Gospel of Christ unless we identify ourselves with those to whom we offer it, and live amongst them, sharing their lives. This is never easy nor free from pain.

If, then, we really care for people, we shall suffer with them in their sufferings, even as Christ Himself suffered for and with us during His life on earth. All this is but another way of saying that it costs to love people. It is something like this that Jesus meant when He said: "For their sakes I sanctify myself."

Love is always difficult to define, but perhaps it can best be described as the giving of oneself, the outgoing of oneself to another, so that in a sense one belongs to the person whom one loves. This oneness which true love makes possible is seen not only in physical love between man and wife and in their deep and intimate belonging to each other, but in a lesser degree it can be seen in all true love. We cannot love anybody without making contact with them; such contact means to some extent a bodily proximity through exchange of looks, of activity, of conversation; but it means, too, so loving that we seek to give ourselves to their minds, to their emotions, and to their inner selves.

This kind of love and self-giving, which is real caring, would be at the very least the kind of love that costs the little extra, or, to use the words of Jesus, goes the "second mile."[11] The first mile, to help the postman to carry the mail bag, according to Roman law was obligatory on any person who was asked; but, says Jesus, do not simply do your legal duty, go all the way, do the extra mile. This is a real mark of Christian living,

[11] Matthew 5:41

the willingness to care enough to do more than we need, than we are obliged to, for other people.

The story of the Good Samaritan illustrates this admirably. The robbers were essentially selfish; that is why they robbed the man and left him, not caring whether he lived or died. The Good Samaritan was essentially unselfish. He went beyond any obligation of race or relationship and got off his ass to help the man in need. The priest and the Levite were not bad men at all; they faithfully fulfilled their legal obligations, but could not be bothered to care enough to do the little bit extra, and go out of their way to help.

This caring love also shares what it possesses. I am not thinking now particularly of the sharing of the Gospel, though this is implied. As Mildred Cable said: "I went out to Tibet because the people there had a right to know that Christ died for them." I am referring rather to the need of every Christian to be a giving Christian, and every church to be a giving church. The Dead Sea is dead, because it takes in but never goes out. For myself I am sure that the principle of tithing as taught in the Old Testament, and in basic principle reaffirmed in the New, had this purpose in mind. If we learn to give to God a proportion of our possessions, this symbolic act will help us to see firstly His claim upon all our possessions, and also to become a giving person who will discover it is "more blessed to give than to receive."

It is strange, perhaps, that the giving of money should release springs of giving within us. It may well be that this is so because to most of us modern people money is a symbol to us of the work we have done to make it our own; it is part of us which we can use to build up our own lives, and all that belongs to us and surrounds us. Thus when our money is given in a genuine, thought-out proportion to God's work we are in the concrete, and not merely in the abstract, giving ourselves to God, or to express it in another way, putting ourselves through our money into circulation in God's service.

This caring love will also lead us to seek to understand. Elsewhere in this book I have referred at greater length to this need to understand our fellow men, but here I want to point out that it is costly really to sympathize and to seek to understand another human being, yet to understand all is to forgive all.

This spiritual discernment is one of the gifts of the Spirit for which Paul prays for himself and for his friends. Such understanding love will make a Christian a reconciling person, one who is able to help others to be right not only with God, but with their neighbors. It is here too that the Christian Church reveals its true self; it is the community of the forgiven, and therefore must show itself as a forgiving community. It is perhaps with this thought in mind that Jesus said a special blessing would rest upon those who are not simply peace-seekers, and looking only for their own convenience and ease, but upon those who at the cost of suffering and caring will become peace-makers. They shall inherit the Kingdom of God, which after all is the kingdom of love.

In this willingness to suffer we shall discover that it is a much deeper experience than mere unselfishness. It is a gradual dying to self that we may live for Christ, and for the "brothers for whom Christ died." It will lead us, not to self-glorification, or to self-gratification that we have been used to help others; we shall find instead a very deep sense of our own inadequacy, a wonder that God uses us at all, and the experience of pain, a travail of soul, that there is so much in God's world which is wrong, that our share in trying to redeem is but a drop in the ocean of need. Yet it will bring us assuredly again and again to that point where, as Peter said (though in different words) by the Sea of Galilee, we in our turn shall sincerely say:

> *Take my love; O Lord I pour*
> *At thy feet its treasure store;*
> *Take myself, and I will be*
> *Ever, only, all for thee.*

CHAPTER VIII

Christlikeness

THE fourth aspect of development in Christlikeness is *the quality of gentleness.* We cannot read the Gospels without noticing how gentle Jesus was, tremendously gentle; not that for a moment I am suggesting the sentimentality so often thought to be expressed by the hymn, "Gentle Jesus, meek and mild"—a picture of a kind, amiable person who is never disturbed, angry or passionate. That is no New Testament picture of Jesus, as all serious readers of the Gospel know; but gentleness was certainly one of His supreme characteristics. He was never pharisaical or censorious. He had time for the weak and the poor. It was said of Him: "A bruised reed shall He not break; a smoking flax shall He not quench." He displayed great tenderness to people nobody else wanted, the unloved and the unlovely. He went out of His way to give His friendship and He gave it with gentleness.

The early Church caught the spirit of its Master, and in the first century this made the Christian community very different from the world around them. Professor Butterfield, as a historian, treats this as very significant: "Christianity must have an influence in every age. Christian teaching contains certain elements which will produce a softening of manners; in the ancient Roman empire it stressed the sanctity of human life, the importance of the family, the evils of sexual licence and divorce, the wickedness of suicide or the gladiatorial contests or the murder of infants. Christianity was standing for a higher estimation of personality, based on the view of man as a spiritual creature. Furthermore the organization of charity was carried by the Christian Church to the point at which we can regard it as an original contribution to the life of the time. In the fundamental place which it gave to love, in its emphasis on gentleness, humility, joy and peace, the Christian was parting from the ethical ideas of the pagan world, and promoting a different kind of personality, a different posture for human beings under the sun."[1]

This gentleness of manners springs from a deep sense of the wonder of God's forgiveness. What should matter most to the real Christian is the fact that Christ received him just as he was; with all his sins and weaknesses he was loved and forgiven. If this is so then how can he be ungenerous to other sinners? In face of God's forgiveness to me I must ask myself: "Who am I not to forgive others?" The Lord's Prayer points out: "Forgive us our trespasses as we forgive them that trespass against us." We who have been really forgiven by God, accepted by Him as we are, must also accept other people and forgive them. I think it is true to say that a man cannot genuinely experience God's forgiveness for himself, and not be himself in his turn a forgiving person. There is something radically wrong with him if he is not. Jesus made this point in His parable about the man who was pardoned for a debt of over a million but who demanded from his neighbor a dollar bill due. The hard, ungenerous, mean attitude was utterly condemned. The hall-mark of Christlikeness is to be a forgiving person. This generosity of spirit, this gentleness of attitude is the supremely important Christian characteristic.

Sometimes I am worried about the world-wide Church; what worries me is that sometimes it does not appear to be the place where above all else true forgiveness abounds. I can understand, and in a way—though do not misunderstand me—I am not unduly perturbed if the Christian Church contains amongst its members adulterers and jealous people and selfish

---

[1] *Christianity in European History,* New York: The Macmillan Company, 1953, p. 14. London: William Collins Sons and Co., Ltd.

people, and all other kinds of sinners, but it does matter terribly if the Christian Church has unforgiving people in its midst, people who call themselves Christians, but who are not gentle and generous toward others, for such people deny the very experience that has made them Christian.

I remember one Sunday night an unmarried lady, a regular member of my congregation, brought to the service with her a married man. His marriage was rather moving toward the rocks, and perhaps his friendship with this other lady was not altogether wise, though there was nothing fundamentally wrong. Before the service began another lady, also a regular member, leant across and said to the first: "You know, you ought not to bring that man in here. He has no right to come to church." How utterly opposed to the spirit of Jesus, who was described as the man who was always receiving sinners!

On the other hand, I remember with happiness a Christian lady who gave a warm welcome and her friendship to a man and a woman who began to worship in my church. This couple had lived together unmarried for seventeen years. They had two children, and were trying to make a real home for them. For many years they had stayed away from the Christian Church, but by chance we made contact with them, and they began to come back again. They could not get married, for his wife was still alive, and there was no divorce. I am not justifying that wrong relationship; it was, from a Christian standpoint, sinful; but what was a real happiness to me was the way in which the member of my congregation welcomed them, made them feel at home in church, and gave them the gentleness of her friendship.

Closely linked with the unforgiving spirit is the censorious attitude which negatives Christian gentleness. Smugness, self-righteousness, complacency, a better-than-thou attitude—these prevent us from showing the generosity toward others which we ought to show. This is a danger which besets many Christian enthusiasts. They are often found in the more evangelical congregations: they are full of evangelistic zeal, and serve the Lord most fervently; they are very keen, and they are very consecrated to Christ, but so often they tend to pass judgement on all their other fellow Christians. They refer to them as the "weaker brethren" who must not be scandalized. They are quite sure in their own minds that *they* themselves could never be a cause of stumbling to anyone. They question the sincerity of the conversion of others, and speak doubtfully of the genuineness of their Christianity. There is a real spiritual danger lurking here. The enthusiasts may sometimes be quite right, and those whom they think are not converted may really not be converted. Often, however, they are showing a censorious spirit, and are lacking in gentleness as well as in spiritual discernment. Sometimes such an attitude casts a doubt on the reality of the conversion of the person who holds it, so that the weaker brethren are actually nearer the kingdom. Is not self-conscious righteousness the one really damning sin?

Many disciples of our Lord who are indeed the salt of the earth are the quite unassuming saints who have a deep love for their Lord, and constantly give themselves in simple, unpublicized selfless service. Many of the best Christians I know would not fit happily in with these fervent evangelists, and yet possess an attractive gentleness which quietly draws many of their friends toward God.

The fifth aspect of development in Christlikeness is the *desire to share the good news*. It cannot escape notice as we read the Gospels that Jesus, wherever He went, talked about God; He was always on His Father's business, telling people about the Father, and trying to bring people to the Father. To put it simply, He sought to share His Father with everyone else.

When a Christian starts growing in Christlikeness he will *desire* to share Christ with others. The word "desire" is important. It is not the case that we must try to screw ourselves up until in an agony of feeling we think we really can say a word for God. This very sentence, and the phrase "word for God" suggests something rather gruesome and unnatural, and quite beside my point. It is much rather along the lines of the Quaker saying: "Never speak unless thou dar'st not keep silence." We ought to be Christians of such a quality that we dare not keep silent. We should be so constrained by the love of Christ that we should be impelled to share Christ as opportunity offers. After all, the knowledge of Christ should be the best experience I have, the best secret I have; if I am friends with anyone I ought to want to share with him my best. This is quite natural and unembarrassing. There should be neither strain here, nor nervous stress. People I know only casually are not people with whom, as a rule, I share my intimate secrets. To such people, while taking every opportunity that naturally offers to bear witness for my faith, I shall not perhaps introduce the subject of personal religion. When, however, I know someone well enough to talk about any subject that crops up then I am beginning to be on a basis of friendship where I can share Christ with him.

Before the Second World War when I was a Vicar in North London I chaired an interesting monthly open-air meeting. The three speakers were a Roman Catholic controversialist, a Congregational minister, and myself. We tried to answer any questions that were thrown at us. I remember on one occasion some Communist hecklers became very angry with us, and accused us of having a specious unity. They shouted: "This unity of you Christians is phoney. Isn't it true that the Roman Catholic speaker wants to make you a Roman Catholic too, so where's the unity?" My answer came straight from the shoulder: "Of course he wants me to be a Roman Catholic, because we happen to be very good friends, and therefore naturally as a friend he wants me to share the best he has got." The Roman Catholic himself added: "That's right. Of course I do; but I also want to add that we have a real unity in that I recognize that he, no less than I, belongs to the mystical spiritual Body of Christ." The point is clear. Real friendship is sharing, and into this sharing comes the sharing of the best I know—the knowledge of Christ.

One of the most disastrous failures in this connection, and one of the most common, is seen in the realm of marriage. I cannot understand how a real Christian can marry someone who is not. More amazing still is the infrequency with which ministers teach and warn against this mistake.[2] A Christian

[2] The Christian principle is clear, even though it does happen occasionally that a man or a woman finds faith in Christ through the love of the married partner.

home is impossible unless both partners are Christians; the sharing of the body can be fully satisfying; the sharing of the mind real companionship; but unless there is also a sharing of the spirit there is something deep and real missing. On this the New Testament is quite clear; on this in theory all Christians would agree; but practice is something very different. The time to start is when a boy and girl, a man and a woman, have begun to become friends. As love begins to develop between them, then is the time for the Christian to share his knowledge of God. It is no argument to say: "I don't want to rush her; I don't want to disturb her; I don't want to push her into believing in Christ because I do." Such an attitude is stupid and wrong. If the man loves the girl at all sincerely he should want to seek to give her the best he has to offer, and that is his faith.

Moreover, the argument that he does not want his girl friend to be influenced toward religion out of love for him is a poor argument. We are often in life influenced out of love for others toward something which is necessary and worth while. Human love can often be the gateway to the discovery of divine love.

My own daughter has a simple and genuine Christian faith, and one of the things I have always respected is her attitude to her boy friends who had little or no religion. She always tried to bring them to church and to win them for Christ. Many a time she has asked me for advice as to how best to answer the questions and difficulties of some agnostic friend. Such an attitude between friends is both sensible and dignified.

I must write plainly. I find it difficult to understand and to respect young people who say they love Christ, and yet never seem to do anything about trying to bring their friends to Him. I know we should not argue from our own experience, yet sometimes we cannot help doing so. When, after a childhood training in Christian things, I came gradually into a real conversion I remember that after I knew that I was Christ's, within a couple of months most of my real friends knew about it. Some did not like it, and a few friends I lost; but to me at that time it was tremendously important that my friends should share what I had experienced, and know what I knew. Looking back, I am sure I was not always wise or tactful, but I was being very natural.

In some ways I would rather have a Christian at the age of nineteen a little too fanatical and over-enthusiastic; as he grows older he will cool down and mature, and in middle life will probably still be a definite and decided Christian. But if at nineteen he is luke-warm and unenthusiastic in his Christian faith, by the time he is middle-aged he will probably have lapsed into indifference and backsliding.

It is a real challenge which middle-aged Christians ought to face if they are seeking to be Christlike. Some of them have not spoken about Jesus Christ to anybody for years. Some have never even spoken to their children about the need to love and to serve Jesus. There will, of course, have been a few remarks about the value of religion, or suggestions that it is a good thing to go to church—but no plain, forthright talking about God and the need for faith in Him. This is a sin, a plain, downright sin, for it is a betrayal of Christ. Christians of all ages, if they really love their Lord and want to share Him, should be on the look-out for opportunities to do so.

I agree that we have got to be wise; we have no right to embarrass others foolishly; there must be a proper propriety; we have no right to intrude ruthlessly into the private life of others. All this is granted. It is also granted that about things that matter much to us we are shy and self-conscious. Perhaps the deeper our love and knowledge of Christ the more sacred and intimate it becomes, so that we find it difficult to share Him. We are afraid, to use the Bible phrase, to cast our pearls before swine lest they be trampled on and sullied. All this is understandable. But the way to deal with this is not by arguments with one's self, and forcing oneself to do one's duty. Self-consciousness disappears when we look away from ourselves, and center our thinking upon the need of our friend, our love for him, our desire for his well-being; and then we can think of Christ and all that He can be to that friend. As we do this we shall find that we are forgetting ourselves, and in the richness of the consciousness of what Christ is and what He can be to others, we shall find ourselves sharing naturally and spontaneously in a way which wins and does not repel; which offers Christ, but does not thrust Him upon the soul of another.

The sixth and final aspect of Christlikeness that I want to notice is *a growth in creative power*. Jesus was never just dully good; He was always creative. I wonder why his friends asked Him to a wedding in Cana of Galilee, and why He accepted the invitation? I am sure He did not go just in order to do a miracle and to turn water into wine. I believe He was asked because His friends wanted Him there; He made a pleasant and happy guest. There are many hints in the Gospels that Jesus was often asked out to dinner, and this is noteworthy—he was often asked to have a meal with sinners and those on the fringe or quite outside the Church. Why did they ask Him? Because, to use our modern colloquialism, He helped to make the party go. When He was present people knew that He was; His personality was sparkling and attractive. It is this aspect of Jesus that I want to consider for a moment.

He had real creative power, and He took hold of situations and people and transformed them; and this is what His Spirit can do for us. We are not given in the teaching of Jesus a hard and fast blue-print for the Christian society, for the kingdom of God. The Koran, I believe, tends to lay down a plan, a code of morals, a fixed standard for living, and that is why its teaching so easily gets out of date; but Jesus gives us no pigeon-holed directions for living. There is no ethical code, all numbered, so that I can look up the appropriate number when I am at a loss to know how to act. There are no stereotyped answers. Christ gives us a spirit with which to face life, not a method with which to solve problems. That is what I mean by creative power.

The Living Christian possessed by the Spirit of Christ need not be pushed about nor broken by the stresses of life. He can react with Christlikeness to all that presses upon him. There is the difference. We may not have a blue-print, but we can have the Spirit of Christ within us to enable us to react Christianly and creatively to all that life brings.

This has always been true in Christian history. Initiative, as well as enthusiasm, has been a mark of Christlikeness. New ideas have sprung into the minds of men led by the Spirit of God, and these ideas have been translated into action. That is what ought to have been happening continually. One of the great tragedies of organized religion, however, is that so often it takes men and women and canalizes their spiritual life and conventionalizes their soul. This is perhaps the damning fact about institutional religion. We have turned out conventional Anglicans, or conventional Methodists, or conventional Evangelicals, or conventional High Churchmen. One of the most important tasks for Christian leadership today, as always, is to allow the disciples of Christ to develop their individuality under the creative guidance of the Holy Spirit.

Perhaps the most tragic illustration of this in my personal experience happened over twenty years ago. An Oxford woman graduate, after some years of agnosticism and very great intellectual struggle, had come into a real Christian experience. It was deeply mystical, and was changing her in a remarkable way. She joined other Oxford students on one of my missions. Once or twice she gave in public her witness to Christ. To hear her was to be greatly moved. There were no Bible words or clichés; she spoke simply and naturally out of her fresh mystical experience. Artistic by temperament, she painted a moving picture of what God had done and was doing for her. It fascinated the hearers by its originality and by its outreachingness.

After one such occasion a fine and most sincere Christian leader came up to me, and pointed out that in her opinion the speaker needed Bible-teaching. "Her theology's all wrong. Unless she gets her ideas straight she will cease to go forward, and will slip back in the Christian life. She ought to go to a Bible School." I was inexperienced, and rather weakly agreed, though not very happily.

My friend went to a Bible College. It was good and it was sound; but in three months she had lost her hardly won faith, and had gone back into an experience of doubt and difficulty. Eight years had to elapse before once more she had recovered her faith, but she never got back the freshness of the mystical experience she once enjoyed. The reason was the attempt, well-meaning, sincere and honest, but wholly misguided, to conventionalize, to standardize, to make sound, yes, even to make biblical, a rich, fresh, individual, inner experience of the Holy Spirit.

I know there is danger here in what I am trying to say, but the work of the Holy Spirit is never safe; in a very real sense it is dangerous. The first Christians were thought to be drunk, and they spoke with tongues and seemed to babble. It was mysterious, disconcerting, did not always seem to make sense; but it was a mighty and real experience of the creative power of the Spirit.

Today when Christians talk they often talk in a petty, trifling way. They do not challenge evil; they discuss and argue about secondary matters; they often seem to have no plan or purpose; they certainly do not thunder out in challenging, startling and dangerous tones the word of God over against the evil of the world. The organized Church is afraid to run risks, and if we prefer conformity and security to enthusiasm and the running of risks, then we can make our choice, but we shall certainly stifle the work of the Holy Spirit. Today visions can be awkward and misleading; but where there is no vision the people perish, and where there is no creative power of the Spirit the Church languishes and falls down on its objective.

Paul tries to give this vision to his friends at Corinth in his second letter. He starts by reminding them that the love of Christ should control them. No longer are they living for themselves; they must live for Him. Has He not done something remarkable for them? They are new people since God reconciled them with Himself through Christ, and through what Christ had done. Now they must live as ambassadors for Christ. God must speak His word to the world through them. By life and lip, everywhere and at all times, they must appeal to the world to turn to God, and to accept salvation in

Christ. Then Paul ends: "As workers together with God" they must seize the opportunity that is theirs.

What a phrase, pregnant with meaning! Christians must be activists. There is no room for drones in the hive of the Church. Here, too, is emphasis on the solidarity of all the redeemed—we are "workers together." Then come the last two words of Paul's phrase—"with God." No doubt it can mean quite properly "with God's help," with the working within us of God's Spirit. Certainly unless this is true we shall do no work of value for God; but I fancy that there is another meaning here. It is a truth which is plainly stated throughout the New Testament, and which is often implicit in much else. The strength of the Marxist philosophy lies partly in the vision it offers to the dedicated Communist. As Willie Gallacher says in his little book *The Case for Communism,* there is an inevitability about the coming of the Socialist State. His book breathes the apocalyptic and messianic spirit of the New Testament, only with God left entirely out. The materialistic secular movement of history will bring in that promised kingdom of the Communist dream. Nothing can stop it. Come it will, and come it must. The true Communist lifts up his eyes to this vision, and then follows the Party line, for to him the Party line means something like this. Whether he lives, or whether he dies, whether he prospers or suffers, no matter; his task and privilege is to co-operate with the Party line, to work with this great movement of history, so that as he co-operates he will have a tiny share in helping to bring about this inevitable result of the movement at the heart of all things. Here is his confidence, and here is his hope.

Paul sees the same kind of vision, only he sees the kingdom of God—a purposeful movement within history, a movement guided by the hand of the living God which will inevitably bring, in God's own good time, the promised kingdom of God and of His Christ. He exhorts his fellow Christians to follow the Christian party line; whether they prosper or whether they suffer, whether they live or whether they die, their task and privilege is to co-operate with the will of God, to play their small part, each of them individually, and all of them together, in helping to bring in God's final purpose for the world.

Here is the Christian's confidence, and here is the Christian's hope. Seeing this vision and yielding himself to the Spirit of God, his life becomes creative with the power of God.

CHAPTER IX

A Life of Fellowship

THE fifth mark of the Christian life is that it is *a life of fellowship,* for in a very real sense there is no such person as a solitary believer. The old Roman Catholic doctrine "There is no salvation outside the Church" is true, though not in the way that it is normally applied. To the Roman Catholic the "Church" means his Church and none other, and therefore the doctrine is affirming that outside the Roman Catholic communion no one can be truly saved, in the sense of finding the fullness of Christian experience here on earth, while in the next life the non-Roman Catholic can find salvation only through the uncovenanted grace of God, and provided he has died in good faith.

If, on the other hand, we use the word "Church" in what is to us the true biblical sense, the universal Body of Christ, then the dogma is a true statement of fact. Outside and apart from the Church man cannot find the Christian experience. If he turns to the Bible then, he is using the Book of the Church; for apart from the Church writing, preserving and translating there would be no Scriptures. Does he look to the Sacraments? They are the Sacraments of the Church, originated within, and passed on through, its life. If he hears the preaching of the Gospel, that proclamation is made by a member of the Church. Only then through contact with, and through eventually coming within, the Body of Christ can an individual find the true salvation which Christ offers.

To put it rather differently. I cannot be a Christian by myself, for at the heart of the Christian faith and practice stands the Holy Communion, the fellowship meal—and I

97

cannot have the Holy Communion by myself. It is a shared feast with other believers.

It is clear, then, that the Christian Church is not simply an extra which I can enjoy if I care to; it is not an optional subject for the examination for Christian proficiency; it is not a club which I can join if I feel inclined to pay the membership subscription. It is, rather, a body to which I cannot help but belong if I am a Christian at all. The biblical phrase, "a man in Christ," does not mean simply someone who personally believes in and shares in the divine life of Christ; it carries also the thought that I share in the life of Christ in and through Christ's Body, the Church.

At Pentecost when the Holy Spirit was given He was given indeed to individuals—"it sat upon each of them," but He came "when they were all with one accord in one place." Now the Church is the incarnate Body of Christ here on earth through which He still lives and works, through which worship is offered to God, and through which He shares His redeeming message to the world, and through which He reveals His divine life to those outside.

When I was born, whether I liked it or not, I was born into the Green family. I may now wish I had been born into the Smiths or Williamses, but it cannot be. I was born a Green and a Green I must remain. Moreover, my family was there before I was born, or else I never could have been born. So it is that the Christian Church, the family of God, gives me new birth into Christ. Without that previous family life I could never have been born into the Christian experience. Now that I am so born I am, whether I like it or not, a member of the family. In this way the individual Christian is inextricably bound up with the Church of God, and because we are members of that Body we are also members one of another, and must realize that fellowship.

If, therefore, it is true that outside the Church there is no salvation then the Christian Church is not simply a fellowship of sociability where we meet like-minded friends, nor is it a club of earnest-minded people who wish to serve the community for Christ's sake, though indeed the Church is both incidentally. It is first and foremost a fellowship or family of those who are saved by the precious blood of Christ, who meet as a community of the redeemed, as a society of the forgiven, with a deep gratitude to their Savior, and a genuine love for each other. From this gratitude, and through this love, they are inspired and strengthened to serve their Lord in the world in which they live.

The expression of such a fellowship is a wide subject, and I can only draw attention to two or three salient points. If we keep this idea of fellowship in our minds then the habit of churchgoing is seen in an entirely different light. What is the motive? It is not that we go to church on Sunday because we think it will help us, or because we feel like it, or because it is good for the children, or because we have been asked to pass round the plate. These are all genuine motives, but the real reason for regular church attendance is plainly and simply because we are members of a family, and our place must not be empty at the family gathering.

The Roman Church often seems to members of the Reformed Churches to have many abuses and distortions of doctrine, but they have some great truths and practices from which we could most profitably learn a lesson. For instance, they plainly teach their people from childhood, as we have seen in a previous chapter, that to miss Mass on Sunday is a mortal sin, it is deadly to the soul to be away from your fellow Christians on the first day of the week when His Body is broken and His Blood shed in the Sacrament. I believe this is perfectly right and symbolic. It is a sin which imperils the soul wilfully to miss the family worship within the Christian Church on the first day of the week. It is our duty to be there, and we have no right to stay away; it is wrong to mutilate the family's worship by our absence.

Here is a conception of the solidarity of believers which would transform our Sunday worship. We should see the whole act as a family act; we should see the need to play our particular part within it; we should not test the value of this worship by whether we feel uplifted and inspired, or whether the sermon is helpful or not; we often should be inspired, and

I hope the sermon often would be helpful; but the real joy and value to us would be that after worship we could look back and say: "I was there, there in my place, part of the whole worshipping body of Christ's faithful people."

This conception of fellowship would also save us from that parochialism which bedevils so miserably the Christian Church. So often one hears of little congregations of Christians refusing even to move their building from some down-town factory area into a developing suburb where thousands of people have no church building, and no openly worshipping Christian community. We see congregations raising thousands of dollars to beautify their own sanctuary, but ignoring completely the needs in Africa or Asia for the very essentials that are necessary for the building and developing of the Christian Church. I am sure the Roman Catholic Church, too, is bedevilled with parochialisms, with diocesan introversion, and other points of narrow-mindedness; but at least her people have a conception of Mother Church, the one same Church throughout the world.

The sinful divisions between the Reformed Churches make it more difficult for our members to grasp the idea of the one Church, yet if we could but grasp and put into practice the implications of this idea of the Christian life as a life of fellowship, then the world-wide Church of Christ would take on a new meaning, and we should see our part within it. Naturally, we should be concerned to heal the outward and visible divisions which keep us apart and make intercommunion difficult, but we should be able to see even now a unity which is greater than our separateness. In Slocum-on-the-Mud, a little village in Suffolk, as Christians we should begin to understand that our mission for Christ is to the whole world; we are His Church, and His Church is world-wide. The implications of this new sense of fellowship for Christian strategy and for Christian stewardship of money are obvious.

Another implication of fellowship is that it would re-emphasize the true meaning of the laity—the people of God. In some branches of Christ's Church the division between clergy and people is too marked. In others, though theoreti-

3717ტ.

cally the minister is only a person with a special function to lead worship, to preach the Word and to administer the Sacraments, in practice too much of the leadership and strategy of the Church is left in his hands. In part this is understandable, and springs not from any slackness or theory, but from the general pressure of life. The minister is the full-time professional; the lay people are, as it were, part-time volunteers, therefore on his shoulders must fall the larger burden of the Church's work.

This may be a part of the explanation, but the situation is none the less unhealthy. I doubt very much whether the Church in the twentieth century will ever regain her true vigor and drive until both ministers and lay people realize afresh that they are linked in an indissoluble fellowship, and are equally members of the family, for on each and all of them lies the responsibility for the life and witness of the Church; together they must shoulder this responsibility, otherwise there can be no advance.

This means a good deal more than merely suggesting that lay men and women take on further responsibility within the Church organization, the church building, and the church activities. It means that Christian lay men and women must see themselves as the Church active and witnessing in their neighborhood, and in every part of their daily lives. They are the Church, and they are responsible for its witness.

There are signs in different parts of the world of an increasing acceptance of this responsibility, and a renewed understanding of fellowship. Nowhere is it more marked at present, perhaps, than in the new emphasis being laid upon the stewardship of money, and the practice of tithing. Certainly in America, the British Commonwealth, and now at last in Britain, this implication of belonging to the Church is being taken to heart.

It is clear that if we really belong to the family, then each of us must be prepared to bear his share of the financial support necessary for the family's life. Right back in the Acts of the Apostles this element of fellowship is clearly seen. The first

Christians brought their possessions and laid them at the Apostles' feet. Paul emphasizes the need to minister to the saints, and he urges Christians to lay aside for this purpose on the first day of the week money, as God had prospered them. Such giving of money, and the offering of our material resources is not to be thought of simply as a way of financing the Church. It is a deeply spiritual matter. Money is the symbol of work done. By the giving of ourselves and our labor, by working upon the stuff of life, we have made our money. In this sense it is part of us, the symbol of ourselves given in work, of our productivity. As we set apart a portion of our money for the work of the Church we are symbolically expressing the dedication of part of ourselves to the service of God. It is, of course, clearly true that all our money, just as all of ourselves, belongs to Christ; if we are His at all, then we are altogether His, but just as the man who says "I can pray any time and all the time," but who never prays at a particular time generally ends up by praying at no time, so it is that the man who says "All that I have is Christ's," but does not bother to dedicate a particular portion of what he possesses to God, ends up by giving very little, if anything.

It is for this reason that fellowship demands that each of us who is a Christian should give thought and care to discovering the proportion of our resources that should be dedicated in a special way to God and to His Church. For some the Old Testament principle of tithing may seem right; for others some other method may be preferable; but for all of us there should be some conscious and deliberate settlement of what we give week by week to the service of Christ and of His Church. Casual and impulsive giving may sometimes seem more generous and more spontaneous, but pledged, regular and thought-out giving is evidence of a truer sense of fellowship and shared responsibility.

These are some of the implications of the Christian life when it is seen to be a life of fellowship—a life in Christ, shared and lived within the unity and as a member of the family of those who belong to the same Lord and who own the same Savior. The purpose of this unity in fellowship is not primarily for our own spiritual strengthening and happiness. It is outward-looking, and is meant to be a witness that the world may know through our oneness, our One Lord and Savior and the One True God.

CHAPTER X

A Life of Discovery

THE sixth mark of the real Christian life is that it is *a life of discovery*. This note is very evident in the New Testament. In the opening words of his letter to the Christians at Ephesus Paul tells his friends that he is praying to God that they might receive "the spirit of wisdom and revelation in the knowledge of him, that the eyes of your understanding being enlightened ye may know what is the hope of his calling, and what the riches of the glory of his inheritance in the saints, and what is the exceeding greatness of his power to us-ward who believe."[1] He echoes the words of the Lord Jesus who promised that the Holy Spirit, "when He is come, shall guide you into all truth."[2]

As we grow in the Christian life we should come to discover something of what it really means to be a Christian, and what are the spiritual resources at our disposal. It will be given to us to know more about God, and more about man. Here is no standing still; here is the glorious adventure of possessing unsearchable spiritual riches, some of which we can always be discovering and appropriating. This is what gives to the Christian experience its freshness. There is nothing static; it is meant to be a moving forward into fresh insights, fresh knowledge, and fresh action.

There is no doubt that this is the climate of the New Testament, but I am not at all sure that it is the climate in which the modern Christian lives. In very many Christian communities the adventure of spiritual discovery seems to be absent. There seems to be no life and movement. Spiritual

[1] Ephesians 1:17   [2] John 16:13

104

fervor seems to be at a low ebb, and individual Christians stationary as regards any progress.

It is, therefore, important to emphasize this note of discovery very early on in the Christian life. In my evangelistic work I naturally meet many who have been privileged to have a dramatic conversion—a definite crisis in the process of their Christian experience. If I have the opportunity of seeing such people a little while after their conversion, I have a question which I always try to ask. I do not say to them, "Do you feel happy? Are you behaving better? Is it lasting?"—but I do ask, "What have you discovered?" Far more important than any feeling of happiness or even than changed behavior is the discovery of something new and fresh about God. If a man has become alive to God through Christ, then he ought to expect to discover and find out more about the spiritual world as the days pass. The Christian life is meant to be a life of continuing discovery.

Some years ago I was asked to meet a brilliant young medical student, a girl of some eighteen years. Her parents never went near a church, and although in her very early teens she herself had gone for two or three years she had given it up from intellectual disbelief of what she heard taught there. She called herself an atheist.

During her early months at the university, being a strong personality, she had tackled some of her Christian friends, and badly confused them. They did not know how to handle her challenge. One day a fellow student, a Methodist, said to her: "I can't argue with you, your are too clever for me, but I bet you would not argue with a parson." Her retort was immediate: "Of course I would, and I would love it."

That was how I came on the scene. For three hours we argued. I certainly failed to convince her, though I was able, being older and more experienced, to expose some of the weaknesses of her position. The chief result was that we became friends. She had a good mind which I respected, and so we met and continued our discussion. In the end we got nowhere, and I concluded our final conversation with words something like these: "Only when God and life break you will you really turn to Him"—and so we said good-bye.

I saw nothing more of her for some seven years, and then late one evening my telephone rang, and my caller asked if I remembered her name. I did not, and said so. Then she reminded me of our argument years before, and went on to ask whether she could come round and see me. The voice was urgent, and fortunately I was free, and so I invited her to come immediately.

When she arrived, and as she walked into the room, her first sentence was: "Do you remember the last words you said to me?" At the time I did not. "Well," she continued, "you told me that God would break me, and He has. Now I need help, and I don't know whether it is a psychiatrist or a parson that I need. I want one or the other, and I have decided to try you first."

As we began to talk I found out that she was a qualified doctor, married, and that much had happened in her life in the intervening years. Now life had broken her. She felt lonely, frustrated, spiritually naked and defenseless, and she wanted God. That night God found her, very simply, very really.

During the next two or three months I saw her quite frequently, and each time I opened our talk with the words: "What have you discovered now?" Every time there was something new she was longing to tell me. On the first occasion this is what she said: "Do you remember what a tiny little bit of faith I had the other night? How very feeble my trust was when I genuinely turned to God? You told me that if I went on from that, to try to obey what God told me to do, my faith would grow. I have discovered that that is true. It is just what has happened." She had never read her Bible before, but now she read it, and the whole picture came alive to her. A fortnight after her conversion she had read right through Luke's Gospel. She produced on a piece of paper a number of questions for me to answer. I found that they were the difficult questions and the difficult passages that were often set for scripture examinations! And so it went on. As she followed Christ in the simple obedience of faith, so she discovered rapidly and amazingly some of the truths about the Christian life and faith.

This is God's intention for all of us who are Christians. We are meant increasingly to know more about God and His character, about Christ and His teaching, and about the Holy Spirit and the way He leads us.

I sometimes have it said to me rather sadly by a Christian man who has been arguing with a Communist that he has found that a genuine Communist knows more about his philosophy and dogma than the Christian knows about his. This is often distressingly true. *Why* is it? It is not necessarily because the Communist has read more books or listened to more lectures on Communism than the Christian has on Christianity. Part of the basic training of a Communist is that he must link learning about Communist theory with Communist action. As he does this he discovers the meaning and application of the theory in practice and in life. He discovers its relevance and meaning. The Christian, so often when he reads the Bible, fails to take its teaching and to obey it in action. It is when he does this that he will discover its meaning, and also will discover new truth.

This idea of discovery applies to other aspects of Christian practice. I remember a man of forty-five asking me about prayer, for, he said, he found his prayers difficult and unhelpful. I agreed with him that prayer would always be difficult, but as he pointed out, it was not just that his prayers were difficult, but they were utterly unreal and unhelpful. "Excuse me asking," I said, "but what do you pray each night?" After a moment of hesitation he blurted out: "Well, as a matter of fact, I only pray what I was taught to pray when I was a child —'Gentle Jesus, meek and mild, look upon a little child.'" "How can that mean anything," I asked him, "to a man of forty-five?" He had never discovered in all these years anything more in prayer. His prayer life had been standing still.

The Bible contains many promises that God will guide His people, and show them the way they should go. For many of us the discovery of God's guiding hand is one of the great joys of our Christian lives. Some lay a good deal of insistence upon the seeking of guidance from God, trying to find out before we make a decision what is the decision He wants us to make. That there is a real truth here I am sure, and certainly in my own experience there have been crises in my life when I needed God's guidance, genuinely sought for it, and, I believe, received it. Yet, on the other hand, there is something even finer and more real than this experience of the guiding hand of the heavenly Father. It was well expressed by a Warden of Keble College, Oxford, in a letter which I had the opportunity of reading. He was writing about guidance. He said that in all his years of Christian experience he had had very few, if any, occasions when he definitely knew of God's guidance before he made a decision. To him it was a case of trying to look at a situation with the mind of Christ, searching the Scriptures for any help that he could find, asking the advice of Christian friends, and in his prayers telling God that he was willing to do what He wanted. Then he had to make his decision and act. "But," he added, "for many years I have kept a diary, and never a year has ended when, reading back over the past twelve months, I have not been humbled and glad to see what I believe is the guiding hand of God upon my life." Here was the discovery of guidance which brought with it confidence and trust concerning what lay ahead.

The Christian also learns to discover the breadth of God's love. As Dr. Faber wrote:

> But we make His love too narrow
> By false limits of our own;
> And we magnify His strictness,
> With a zeal He will not own.
> For the love of God is broader
> Than the measures of man's mind,
> And the heart of the Eternal
> Is most wonderfully kind.

This is a discovery of great importance and practical value. In the early days of our Christian experience many of us tend to be somewhat narrow and dogmatic. Soundness in the faith means agreement with our own views. We find ourselves easily able to divide Christians up into the keen, the not so keen, and the dead. We put our fellow believers into categories of one kind and another. This perhaps does not do much harm in the early days, but unfortunately there are many who do not grow out of this narrowness through spiritual discovery. The advancing years do not mature and broaden their Christian understanding. Others discover the variety of God's ways with man. This may be a dangerous experience, but it is exciting and full of interest. Let me give one or two examples of what I mean.

Many Christians have looked at the people of other religions as if there is for them nothing real in the way of a knowledge of God, or of true spiritual experience. All that they believe is evil; their worship is false and idolatrous. Other Christians have discovered as they have come to understand God better that the God they know in Christ is a self-disclosing God; at the very heart of His being lies a forgiving love which for ever makes Him want to reveal Himself to all men everywhere. The discovery of this great fact about God's nature opens our eyes. We begin to realize that if God is like this, a self-disclosing God, then He is, and always has been, seeking to disclose Himself to men everywhere.[3] We should, therefore, expect to find amongst people of other religions here and there those who have caught a glimpse of God's self-disclosure, who have had some real spiritual insight, and who have had some genuine spiritual experience. True, it is not the full under-standing and knowledge of God as revealed in Christ, but it is a real experience of God. This makes a very great difference to our attitude to the great religions of the world, and to our relationships with those who practice them.

The other example is somewhat similar. The fuller discovery of God's nature in Christ makes me question the definitions of Christian dogma. Whereas before I was able to express my faith in simple black-and-white propositions, now I see this man-made formula to be only an approximation of what

[3] Romans 2:14,15; 1:19,20

vaguely I know, and the Christian Church knows, by experience about God. It is not that I throw over the great affirmations of the Christian Creeds—I hold to them still, and genuinely believe them; but I see them as human expressions of great, ineffable truths, as feeble approximations which cannot really express or contain what they try to say. True, this can produce an attitude of doubt which inhibits a clear and firm proclamation of the Christian faith, but it need not do so. It should, rather, lead to maturity of Christian thinking and expression, and to a deep and genuine sympathy with the sincere agnostic, and for those on the fringe of the Christian Church who would like to believe, but cannot.

To sum up, let me underline my main point here. This maturity or mellowness of Christian experience is not the result primarily of intellectual broadmindedness, nor is it the product of conscious effort. It springs, as I have suggested, naturally and spontaneously from a continual and fresh discovery of the nature of God and His ways with men.

In the Psalms there is a lovely phrase which reads: "All my fresh springs are in thee."[4] The Holy Spirit will work in my life to give me fresh springs, fresh discoveries, fresh understandings and insights of God. Jesus meant much the same when He said: "If any man thirst, let him come unto me, and drink. He that believeth on me, out of him shall flow rivers of living water."[5]

[4] Psalm 87:7 (PBV)
[5] John 7:37–8

CHAPTER XI

A Life of Freedom

THE seventh mark of the Christian life is that it is *a life of freedom*. Whatever else the Christian life is it is not primarily one to be lived under a series of rules and regulations. We are not under law, but we are under grace. Paul was always very clear about this, and the whole Epistle to the Galatians is largely a treatise upon this point. The Christians in Galatia had found the free forgiveness of God, and were rejoicing in their new experience of forgiveness and acceptance in the Beloved. Then the legalizers arrived, and tried to force them both to conform to certain ritual acts and ceremonies, and to accept the legal requirements of the Old Testament; all this above and beside the moral law which was fulfilled in Christ, and which the Galatian Christians gladly sought to obey. To them Paul gave his clarion call: "Stand fast in the liberty wherewith Christ hath made you free."[1] He goes on to say that in one sense there are no binding rules or commandments which are obligatory for Christians. We must resist the ever-present temptation that, having become Christians through simple faith in Christ and all He has done for us, we now seek to maintain our Christian life by the keeping of moral laws. "Through the Spirit," he continues, "we wait for the hope of righteousness . . . faith working through love."[2] This is the great law, the one law, for the Christian, the law of love, for "love is the fulfilling of the law." In saying this, however, he is saying something tremendous, because there is no such thing, correctly speaking, as free love. Love is the most binding force on earth.

[1] Galatians 5:1   [2] Galatians 5:5 (*RSV*)

Here is a daughter going to Canada, let us say, for a year. She and her mother are devoted to each other. From one point of view it would be much easier for the girl, perhaps, if her mother gave her a list of twenty rules to keep if she was to be a dutiful daughter, pleasing her mother. That would leave the girl quite free to do anything she liked outside the ground covered by the twenty rules. But love is more binding than that. The mother gives her no rules, yet in the girl's mind and heart there is a consciousness of what would please her mother and what would not. This knowledge is inconvenient, for it covers the whole of life, both the known and the unknown situations, both the present and the future. Because she loves her mother she will always find the challenge and standard for her actions. She lives under love, and not under law.

So it is with the Christian life. Our main purpose, put quite simply, is to please God, or to put it in a more specifically Christian way, to please Christ. That is an enormously big task; there is no end to it, and there is no escape from it, if we really love Him.

From this point of view the Sermon on the Mount, for instance, becomes not a series of moral laws which must be kept exactly and explicitly, but an expression of the ideal life for man as Jesus sees it—the kind of human living that would please Him and make Him happy. If, therefore, we love Him we shall seek to live that kind of life, not because it is an obligation commanded, but because it is a life that would please Him.

The Ten Commandments are binding upon the Christian in a similar fashion, not just as the law of God laid down which if we keep we have done our duty, but as a moral law which expresses the nature and character of God whom we seek to serve. Because these commandments help to make the world the kind of world that God wants, we must keep them out of love for Him, and because loving Him we seek to carry out His purpose in the world.

Is this just an academic argument, or does it really make a difference to think like this? I believe it does. In the first place our main question is: "What will please God? How can I express my love for Christ?" Sometimes in life it may seem impossible exactly to keep one of the commandments or exactly and fully to live up to some ideal of the Sermon on the Mount. We may find ourselves in a situation in which we are so involved that any action we take falls short of the ideal. We still can test ourselves by our love for Christ. What in these circumstances, with these commandments and these ideals in our minds, will please Him best? We act then as an expression of our love for Him, though conscious of our failure to be perfect. He sees the offering of this love, and accepts it.

From another point of view this thought is a help. Seeking to please God is so great a task that if I am sensitive to what it means I shall know that I never can properly be well-pleasing in His sight. As Jesus pointed out to His disciples, when all is done we are still unprofitable servants. This means that part of the experience of Christian living is to have an ever-deepening sense of sin. We are always failing, and always will. Yet even as we know this we can rejoice in the fact that we are loved and forgiven by Him whom we fail perfectly to please. We know we love Him, though, with Peter, we hardly dare to say so.

This freedom from law and regulations is not licence, for most certainly it is not a freedom to do just what I like. Paul realized the danger of this misunderstanding when he wrote: "You were called to freedom, brethren; only do not use your freedom as an opportunity for the flesh, but through love be servants of one another."[3] Our freedom from rules needs certain checks if we are to live within the law of love. It is, as I have already written earlier in this book, freedom within a fellowship.

What, for instance, do we mean as Protestant Christians when we claim the right of private judgement? We certainly do not mean that every individual Christian can think just what he likes, and that his view is as true as that of anyone else. This is the false charge that the Roman Catholic often

[3] Galatians 5:13 (RSV)

brings against us. "Look," he argues, "at your Protestant Churches. Everyone can think what he likes. Look at the mess you are in about doctrine, all your differences of views and differences of practice. What you need is to return to a Church which with authority will tell you what to think and how to act. You claim that you go to the Bible for your views. Well, it seems to me as if there are as many views as there are words in the Bible, judging by the results. You need an authoritative Church which will tell you the true interpretation of the Bible. Then, and then only, will you get uniformity, and have a faith which everyone will accept, and a Christian life which everyone can practice."

This is the charge, and to it we must make a reply. First, we must admit that there is some truth in what is said. Some Protestants think and teach just as they individually choose to think and teach; but that is not what we mean by the right of private judgement. As a member of a human family each of us possesses within the family circle the right of private judgement. As an adult member we are ultimately free to think as we like, but not just casually or egotistically. If we are a real member of the family it is natural to pay careful regard to what the family thinks, to the atmosphere of the family life, to the practices and habits which make the family what it is. Then, and not until all this has been considered, is it our inalienable right to exercise our private judgement, to form our views, and to make our decisions.

This is no academic illustration. Some of us know to our joy the experience of seeing a child grow up in the family circle to adult life, and using private judgement in just this kind of way. She will be different a little from her parents both in views and practice, but there is a genuine similarity in her outlook and behavior to that of the family in which she grew up. So it is in the Christian family. My private judgement can and must be exercised, but not without a real sharing of the life of the Christian family. This sharing will mean that I am forced to pay careful regard to what the Church thinks, not merely to the present thinking of the Church and to the Christian public opinion of the moment, but to the heritage of the past, to what the Church has been thinking for two thousand years. For example, in reading the Bible I must not say of a passage: "I think it means this or that." Before I come to a conclusion I must ask: "What has the Church thought about this passage since it was first written? What do the scholars think it means?" Then, and not till then, I exercise my private judgement. Sometimes I may be right in repudiating the whole experience of the tradition of two thousand years of Christianity; sometimes I may be right, and the whole Church wrong; but this is most unlikely. Yet it does seem to be part and parcel of the genuine Christian experience that this inalienable right of private judgement should be asserted as part of the freedom of the Christian.

It is not only about what we think, but about how we act, that we have this right of private judgement. The privilege of conscientious objection is a Christian privilege, and we must be prepared to take our stand even to the point of martyrdom. But once again, we must recognize the public opinion of the Christian Church, and the accumulated wisdom of the past. It can only be in rare cases that the individual Christian is right and the whole Church wrong. For instance, there is no law that forces each Christian each day to say his prayers, but Jesus prayed regularly, and for two thousand years Christians have done the same. My private judgement leaves me free either to pray daily or not to pray, but it is not likely that I am behaving properly if I repudiate this accumulated experience and decide that I can manage without private prayer.

History is full of examples of the way in which this matter of private judgement has worked. There have been many cases where the single prophet has had a clearer insight into God's will than the Church of his day, and has stood out alone, and suffered for it. There will always be such occasions, and the freedom to be Christian as we see we ought to be Christian is a possession we should never give up.

One last example from within the Anglican Church. From time to time the Convocations—the Assemblies of clergy within the Church of England—pass what are called "Acts of Convocation." They concern matters of doctrine, of worship, and of morals. They rightly carry great weight, because they are the considered judgement of learned men, and are passed after careful consideration and sincere prayer. They are not, however, hard and fast binding rules upon any member of the Church of England, whether clergyman or layman. We can judge them to be wrong without spiritual peril, but we cannot ignore them easily or lightly. Humility would suggest that the individual clergyman or layman is more likely to be wrong in his judgement than Convocation; he will therefore give great weight and careful thought to these Acts. But in the last analysis he must exercise his own freedom of judgement, and if he disagrees then he must refuse to conform—and then he must be willing to suffer the usual penalty of being a nonconformist.

To sum up: Christian freedom gives me the position where I stand before God Himself answerable to Him alone, yet in humility I must give due consideration and weight both in my thinking and behavior to what is the general public opinion of Christendom. In estimating this I must bear in mind not only the teaching of the Bible, but the tradition of the past, of Christian history. I must open my mind to be influenced not only by academic argument and thought, but by the spirit of Christian worship, and the accumulated experience of Christian living. Then I am free, free to obey my conscience, to exercise my private judgement, and to stand fast in the liberty wherewith Christ hath made me free.

Christian freedom is both dynamic and purposive. It is not only "freedom from" or "freedom in." It is primarily "freedom for" God's service. We are to be released from all bondage that all our powers and the deeps of our personality may be set free to be given gladly and used fully by Him who has made us free.

CHAPTER XII

A Life of Moral Struggle

THE eighth mark of the Christian life is that it is *a life of moral struggle*. Scholars have argued a good deal about the seventh chapter of the Epistle to the Romans. Is Paul here describing his experience before or after he became a Christian? It is the story of a man conscious of a continual conflict going on within his soul. Deeply, at the center of him, he accepts the law of God and longs to do it, yet he knows there is another principle at work within him, a sinful and evil principle which again and again seems to overcome his deepest desires and longing for holiness. In the agony of the conflict he cries out: "The good that I would I do not; but the evil which I would not, that I do. . . . O wretched man that I am! who shall deliver me from the body of this death?"[1]

I think the body of opinion is in favor of this experience of Paul's being a post-Christian one. It is the moral struggle which, as every Christian knows, continues throughout the Christian life. This view is somewhat confirmed by what Paul writes in Galatians, Chapter 5, where having compared the works of the flesh with the harvest of the Spirit he makes the statement: "The flesh lusteth against the Spirit, and the Spirit against the flesh; and these are contrary the one to the other, so that ye cannot do the things that ye would."[2] Though this moral struggle is a fact that Christians must face, the experience of the eighth chapter of the Epistle to the Romans is the characteristic Christian note.

What is this spiritual struggle of which Paul writes, and for that matter, all the other writers in the New Testament? The

[1] Romans 7:19,24   [2] Galatians 5:17

flesh and the spirit are opposite the one to the other. We must understand clearly that he does not mean by the "flesh" our bodies. There have been those within the Christian Church, and there are still some, who seem to think that the body with all its appetites and instincts is evil in itself, that there is something inherently bad about the body. This is a form of an ancient heresy, and is not Christian truth. We are God's creation, and we are both body and spirit. Whatever we think of God's creation, whether by a special act or by evolutionary process, we must conclude that our body is in itself good; God has created it. My instincts and appetites can be distorted and warped, but in themselves they are good. This point can be supported also by the fact of the Incarnation. When the Word was made flesh, He became *our* flesh, He took *our* human body, He manifested Himself to the world through *our* human appetites, instincts and characteristics.

This fact that the human body, and our human mental faculties, are in themselves good is important, and if not clearly grasped can lead to unfortunate consequences. In the struggle for holiness, for instance, there have been those who have thought of fasting and mortification of the body as the drastic dealing with something that is evil in itself, whereas the true idea should be to regard the discipline of the body as a control of the physical part of us so that it shall be a better vehicle for the true expression of our thought and spiritual insight. We discipline a horse that we may ride him the better, not because the horse is bad in itself. There are still some Christians who seem to think that they ought not to enjoy bodily pleasures, that there is something wrong in the love of rhythm, in pleasure in eating, and in other joys which give bodily satisfaction. An extreme case is that of a young Christian man who thought it was wrong to play games, but added that he played tennis because it was good for his health; or another who believed dancing was sinful, and yet danced from time to time so that he might try to win the girl he danced with to a faith in God. Frankly, I should not like to be the girl, nor should I like to play tennis with that man! Somewhere in the mind in both these instances is an inner feeling, a hangover of some misguided idea that the body and bodily pleasure are evil in them-selves.

To take a more important instance, Roman Catholic theo-logians and some others hold that sexual intercourse between husband and wife is only legitimate when practiced for the express purpose of the procreation of children. It is wrong to have the bodily pleasure and sexual feelings of intercourse just for themselves alone. The beauty and meaningfulness of the act itself as a sacrament of the real belonging of love is there-fore wrong as an end in itself, but right only if it is the means to something else. I believe that this moral dictum is based on a faulty theology of the body. It seems to me that all bodily desires and activities are good in themselves, and thus sexual intercourse is a beautiful, meaningful act if expressing true love and a deep personal relationship. Such instincts can, of course, be used selfishly or without meaning and purpose, and thus become wrong, but it is in their abuse and not in their natural use that the sin lies.

Having cleared away the necessary identification of the New Testament word "flesh" with the body, we can ask what does it mean? The best definition is probably "the self," the old self-centered life in which everything is looked at from the egoistic viewpoint. When a man puts himself in the center of his own life, when everything is looked at from the point of view of our own advantage, when life is based on self-interest, when in fact I am the center of my being, then we are describing basic self-centeredness, or the old self-life, the flesh. In this connection it is instructive to notice that what we would call "spiritual" sins, such as envy, pride, and so on, Paul labels as "of the flesh" so that the most carnal thing is conscious spirituality. No wonder Paul was hated!

So deep-rooted is our self-centeredness that we even think and believe we can run our life without God. That is the true Bible definition of the root of sin. It is clear that flesh in this sense is absolutely opposed to the new life in Christ. The self-centered and the God-centered life are opposites. When a man finds a new relationship with God through Christ he begins a new life, a spiritual life centered round Christ, but the old life, self-centered and egoistic, is still in the experience of his personality.

It does not matter whether we describe these opposites within the Christian personality in psychological terms or in biblical phrases. There is this dichotomy in the Christian soul, and the two principles of life are contrary the one to the other. The result is a continual moral and spiritual struggle. That is why it is never easy or comfortable to live the Christian life. There is no room for spiritual or moral laziness. The negro spiritual sings truly: "You can't get to heaven in a rocking-chair; My Lord won't have any lazybones there." The struggle is costly and continuous.

This moral struggle is made all the more difficult and intense by the fact that though the Christian is not of the world he must needs live in the world amid the conditioning processes of modern life. Press, radio, television, business, shops and things to buy, standards of life, society and friends—all these tend to focus upon our desire to get and to have; they tip the scales of living in the direction of self-centeredness and self-interest. God and the spiritual dimension are almost entirely absent.

We cannot help being affected by these conditioning processes. We are caught in the stream of them. It is this that makes the struggle of the spirit so hard. The way to fight in the struggle is not so much to oppose the evil in order to try to crucify the flesh, but rather to open our lives to spiritual influences, and to discover the expulsive power of a new affection. Instead of trying to destroy our self-centeredness, it is better through union with God to allow Christ to become the new and real center of our living.

The secret here may seem obvious, but many Christians miss it. Learning to open one's heart and to submit one's will to the work of the Holy Spirit is infinitely more successful as a way of victory in the struggle than nerving oneself up to fight against what one knows to be wrong. It is possible to see the truth of this line of argument in a very human instance. It always amazes me when I see it, and fills me with joy and thankfulness.

Here is a young girl, modern in outlook, well educated,

earning good money. She has a satisfying job, and many friends. She is a girl of high standards, full of *joie de vivre*. She exercises her opportunities to the full, travels abroad for her holidays, sees things and meets people. Then she meets the man she loves. She gives up her job, goes travelling no more, but settles down to married life. She adapts herself to housework, and does all the chores without grumbling. Quite magnificently she achieves the change, and fits in with serenity and happiness to the life of a married woman. How does she do it? It certainly is not because every morning she makes up her mind to renounce travel, to fight the longings for the old life, to push down selfish and indolent desires. It is rather that there has come into her life a new love—a love for him, and then a little later on a love for them—and it is this love which enables her to win the struggle over the old life, and to enter gladly into the new. It is, we must notice, a struggle, perhaps for some easier than for others; there are the old longings and there are the selfish desires, there is a wish for pleasure and travel, but the new love makes her more than conqueror.

So it is that the love of Christ constrains us, and the Holy Spirit leads us, and as this happens the old things will begin to fall away, and the moral struggle will begin to show signs of victory, until in the end all things become new.

CHAPTER XIII

A Life of Humility

THE ninth and final mark of the Christian life is that it is *a life of humility*. By humility I do not mean absence of conceit; conceit in itself can be a minor sin, though it is unpleasant to others and disturbing to oneself; it is a stupid habit of mind and outlook rather than a major sin. I am reminded of the amusing story, probably apocryphal, of the Roman Catholic girl making her confession. She went regularly once a week. "Father," she confessed, "I am sorry to say I have to confess the same sin again this week. It is my worst sin, and I can't get over it. It is a terrible sin, and I am very ashamed of myself. I must tell you, Father, it is the sin of conceit. I am always thinking of myself as so very good looking." "My child," replied her confessor, "that is not a sin, it's a mistake." The girl left the confessional furiously angry, we are told.

No, humility is not an absence of conceit. Bishop Gore defined it like this: Humility is seeing myself at my true value, others at their true value, and God at His true value. It is when I see myself as I am, and God as He is, that I become really humble. It is not connected, you will observe, with conceit at all. It is connected with pride, the deadliest of the seven deadly sins. Humility is beautifully expressed by Paul when he wrote: "By the grace of God I am what I am." He put no value upon the accident of his birth, his strict religious upbringing, his fervent enthusiasm, all his other natural and cultural advantages. From one point of view they were valuable, but not to Paul as he thought of his Christian experience. What mattered there was that Christ loved him and gave Himself for him, and that forgiveness, free and gracious, was offered to him.

I am humble when in the depths of my consciousness I know that if I am a Christian at all it is because of God's love to me in Christ; it is His free and undeserved favor that has made me what I am; then I can say with the utmost truth: "It is not I, but Christ that liveth in me." Humility is the natural product of justification by faith. When a man realizes that he is utterly unworthy of God's acceptance, God's forgiveness, God's friendship, and then comes to know that all this can be his, utterly and only because Christ died for him, that everything that he knows of the experience of God is a free gift, that this free gift in no way depends upon his own efforts or his own merits, when he realizes that the Christian life can never be self-made, but that it has to be God-given, then within such a man is born the humble spirit and the contrite heart. With true meaning he can express the experience of his soul in the words: "Nothing in my hand I bring, simply to thy cross I cling."

This note of humility is the undertone of the real Christian's thinking and living. It is usually possible to detect it by the way a Christian talks and worships. As a rule, in talking of his religion he does not emphasize his "continued loyalty to Christ to whom he gave himself at Confirmation"; he does not speak much about his "commitment" or "personal dedication" to God's service. He talks rather, if he is sharing intimately his religious thinking, about his continuing acceptance of God's forgiveness—"I always need that"; he stresses his constant need to receive the help of God's Spirit. Notice the difference—not "my dedication," "my loyalty," "my commitment," but "receiving what He gives," "accepting the forgiveness He offers."

I remember once, many years ago, at a religious convention listening to an interesting demonstration of the point that I am making. There must have been well over a thousand young people at this particular meeting, and a young man and a young woman gave their testimonies. Both, I am sure, were real Christians, but only one had humility. The first, an Oxford graduate, spoke of his past life and his moral failures; then told how he confessed his sins, sharing them with a friend and then telling them to God; how he made an absolute surrender; then how his life was changed; how he put this right and put that right.

It was all very true, genuine and convincing. I do not doubt for a moment the truth of his conversion.

Then a young woman, a brilliant surgeon, spoke. Her life, too, had been one of irreligion and of moral failure, but her emphasis was that when she knew her need for God and a different life she could do nothing about it. Then she heard the story of the Gospel, the wonder of Christ's love and His death for her sins, the offer of God's forgiveness; simply she told how she came to God and asked for His forgiveness, and received the gift of new life. Her story was utterly centered in Christ and what He had done, and what He was doing for her. Humility and gratitude were the keynotes.

Humility, then, springs from a conviction of my utter dependence upon God, and that I am nothing except as He makes me something. It is no longer *my* faith that is of importance, but the object of faith that counts. This is true of the way in which a man enters into the experience of justification; it is just as true of the way in which he continues to live the Christian life. "As ye have therefore received Christ Jesus the Lord, so walk ye in Him."[1] By faith I received Christ as my Savior and Lord, my heart crying out to Him: "Lord, forgive me; I don't deserve anything; take me as I am." Thus I took the Savior by faith; so I must walk and live the Christian life by the same faith. At its heart the Christian life is a life of simple trust in God day by day, receiving as a little child all that God wants to be to me. That is why Jesus constantly stressed the need for a simple, childlike faith. Each day He means us, as it were, to stand before Him saying: "Lord here am I. Be to me today all that you want to be as a Savior, as a Friend, as a Guide, as a Master." When this is a spontaneous and continuous attitude our lives will become Christ-centered because we are looking utterly toward Him all the time in trustful humility.

There is a delightful fable about the ocean. The sea, it is imagined, was one day feeling discontented. Disillusioned, it hated living at its low sea level when above it were drifting some delightful little white clouds scudding along before the

[1] Colossians 2:6

wind. The sea grumbled to itself: "I don't see why I should be living down here at this low level. Why can't I live higher up, up there where the clouds are?" And so in its discontent and anger the sea began to lash itself into fierce high waves, flinging the foam of its spray high into the air, yet always it fell down again to the same low level of living. Then one day the sun smiled down on the sea and said kindly: "You want to live on a higher level? Then don't fret yourself, strain and struggle. Lie still and look up." So the sea lay still, very still, and looked up. A warm wind arose, and the sun came down and carried some of the water up nearer to heaven, and presently there were seen some fresh white clouds moving overhead.

If we genuinely desire to live on a higher level of Christian life it is useless to strain and strive to reach heaven. Our business is to lie still and to look up to Christ, and then His Spirit will lift us up, enabling us to live a fuller and better Christian life.

An old-fashioned chorus that I learnt as a child expresses the same idea:

> *Moment by moment I'm kept in thy love,*
> *Moment by moment I've life from above;*
> *Living for Jesus, thy promise divine,*
> *Makes me quite certain, dear Lord, I am thine.*

And this prayer asks God to live out His life in us:
"O Lord, take our minds and think through them; take our lips and speak through them; take our lives and live out thy life; take our hearts and set them on fire with a love for thee; and guide us ever by thy Holy Spirit. Through Jesus Christ our Savior."